What people are saying about …

GodStories

"Andrew Wilson helps us grasp more of God's character and his greatness, guiding us in God's wisdom to lead our lives to his glory. This is a fascinating book that makes the Bible and its author both accessible and vibrantly alive—if you want to know God better, I thoroughly recommend it."

Mike Pilavachi, founder of Soul Survivor

"Andrew Wilson is a remarkably gifted writer and Bible teacher with a solid understanding of Christian theology, and in *GodStories* he repeatedly uses fascinating examples from contemporary science, business, history, cinema, and just plain ordinary life to bring the entire scope of the Bible's teaching to life in refreshing new ways."

Wayne Grudem, PhD, research professor of theology and biblical studies at Phoenix Seminary

"Stories are the language of humanity and the primary language of Scripture. But somewhere in our attempts to distill only the principles, we've lost the narrative art so prevalent among God's people for thousands of years. Andrew Wilson is bringing it back. With insight grounded in orthodoxy and the manner of a friend over coffee, Andrew arrests our attention and captures our imagination.

Perfect as a primer and rich as a reminder, *GodStories* will make you fall in love with the living Word all over again."

Glenn Packiam, author of *Secondhand Jesus*, associate pastor at New Life Church

"Andrew Wilson has a gift for telling stories of the Bible in a way that brings fresh perspective, while staying right in tune with the heart of God. It reminds you of the power of God's story as a whole, and empowers you to tell that story as you live out yours."

Travis Taylor, songwriter/recording artist, director of worship at Calvary Church of Pacific Palisades, California

GOD*STORIES

Explorations in the
Gospel of God

. . . . . .

ANDREW WILSON

transforming lives together

GODSTORIES
Published by David C Cook
4050 Lee Vance View
Colorado Springs, CO 80918 U.S.A.

David C Cook Distribution Canada
55 Woodslee Avenue, Paris, Ontario, Canada N3L 3E5

David C Cook U.K., KingswayCommunications
Eastbourne, East Sussex BN23 6NT, England

The graphic circle C logo is a registered trademark of David C Cook.

LCCN 2009903908
ISBN 978-1-4347-6539-0

© 2009 Andrew Wilson

The Team: Melanie Larson, Amy Kiechlin,
Sarah Schultz, Jack Campbell, and Karen Athen
Cover Design: Mark Prentice
Cover Image: iStockphoto

Printed in the United States of America
First Edition 2009

5 6 7 8 9 10 11 12 13

091014

For Ezekiel Jack Wilson
I love you even more than I thought I would!

Contents

Act Three: Poets and Prophets

Act Four: Jesus and Rescue

ACKNOWLEDGMENTS

Sometimes I feel like the guy who stands on top of the human pyramid in those halftime displays. I mean, I'm only here because I'm standing on the shoulders of dozens of people who won't get their names on the cover or even suggest that they should. Even if I wrote twenty pages of thanks, I still wouldn't cover everyone who has contributed to the book you're now holding. But there are a number of people who, for their huge encouragement and support, deserve special mention.

I start with the Canadians and Americans who opened their homes to Rachel and me in the middle of a freezing winter while this book was being written. Specifically, our thanks go to everyone at The Meeting Place, Fredericton: Joe and Angela Crummey (for the introduction to Second Cup and sorting out a car), Gary and Barb Gallant (for a bed, homemade beer, and protection from the moose), Hugh and Krista Hicks (for the Super Bowl and supper), Kevin and Marilyn Calhoun (for remaining calm), and particularly Carol Macdonald, who showed us remarkable hospitality as well as an astonishing way to get out of a snowdrift. I am also extremely grateful to John and Kim Lalgee and family, who hosted me in the Midwest and encouraged me more than they know, both about churches and children. My thanks to you all.

On the production side, I am very grateful to the team at Survivor and David C. Cook, who have turned my scribblings into a real book. Les Moir, Richard Herkes, Don Pape, and Terry Behimer have all been remarkably patient and supportive, Mel Larson translated me into language that Americans could understand (although some phrases, such as "small enough to fit in a boot of a Mini," were beyond even her!), and I dread to think how many phone calls Paul and Sally Johnson have fielded between them about all sorts of things, remaining helpful and upbuilding throughout. Each of these people have gone way beyond what could be expected of them, especially in the final stages, and my profound appreciation goes out to each of them.

Then there's the army of friends in the UK who have shaped the book by their encouragement, input, prophecies, and prayers—Judith Barnett, Terri Belsey, Simon Brading, Dave Dean, Jez Field, Matt Giles, John Groves, Chris Hartingdon, Graham Marsh, Chris Mason, Alice Ovenden, Nikki Petty, Wendy Stevens, Mick Taylor, Andy Thorpe, Simon Virgo, and most of the students and twenties at Kings Church Eastbourne (www.KingsChurch.eu), other than Jo and Rachel Pavey. Three people in particular e-mailed me with very useful resources when I was in a fix—Andy Johnston, Mark Driscoll, and the aforementioned Sally Johnson—and *GodStories* is much stronger for their input. Mike Gilbert produced a quite brilliant animation for the Web site, www.GodStoriesBook.com, which has been both an outstanding worship resource and an extremely generous gift. Underlying all of that, this book would have been both spiritually and physically impossible without the generosity and unwavering levels of support I have received both from my parents, Charles and Julia Wilson, and from my in-laws, Richard and Jenny James:

flights, decoration, babysitting, and most importantly, four lives lived pursuing God and his story. And I would like also to thank two people whose influence is all over the book, even though they may not realize how much: Reuben Lyons, for giving me the whole idea of GodStories in the first place, and Phil Moore, for his remarkable commentaries, example, faith, and friendship. It is people like these who, when I'm standing on top of the human pyramid, make sure I don't fall.

But only one person stands at the top of the pyramid with me. While I've been writing this book, Rachel has endured Nigerian summers, Canadian winters, transatlantic separation, and stolen laptops, all the while editing the text, coming up with chapter ideas before breakfast, and giving birth to our amazing son, Zeke. "I'm thankful" somehow doesn't quite feel adequate to the most beautiful and entertaining person I know. Neither does "I love you." But I am, and I do. Thank you for being you.

PROLOGUE

Several years ago in northern Nigeria, Emily was strung up on a tree and left for dead because she had epilepsy.[1] Her tribal village had no idea what epilepsy was, let alone how to cope with it, so they tied her up and left her there, waiting for her to die from starvation or exposure. Just before she did, Daniel arrived with a small team to preach the gospel and plant a church. Horrified, he immediately cut down the young girl from the tree and put her under a doctor's care. Then he and his team began explaining the gospel to the villagers.

Daniel has paid a price for his zeal. He, his wife, and his children have experienced pretty much every suffering you can have for preaching the good news: robbery, rape, physical beatings, death threats, the lot. But that hasn't stopped him. In fact, from the little I have seen, his sufferings have increased his determination to establish churches and train leaders.

But as people in the village started responding to the gospel, Daniel and his team were able to plant a small church, and then build a school to educate the children. Daniel understood GodStories, you see. He had gone to the village in the first place because he knew the GodStory of world mission. He knew that he would face serious persecution for preaching the gospel, but he knew the GodStory of Christ's suffering and was prepared to share it. When he got there, he preached GodStories about the gospel of God concerning his Son, victory over demons, and the death of death. He started bringing health care and education to the community because he knew GodStories about God's kingdom, man in his image, and the renewal of creation. I've had the privilege of seeing the results firsthand: There is a thriving church in the village, nearly two hundred children at school every day (their English grammar is better than mine!), and Emily is still alive. Because of Daniel's conviction that the gospel story is amazing, hope has conquered despair in that community.

And he certainly won't stop preaching GodStories. Maybe it's because he knows how they all end.

The Greatest Story Ever Told

The point of this book is to convince *you* that the gospel is amazing. It's aimed at anyone who wants to understand the good news of what God has done: teenagers, caretakers, businesspeople, full-time mothers, artists. Knowing the gospel is the foundation for worship and mission, so the only thing we're going to do in this book is explore the beautiful, triumphant, often-heartbreaking, and always-glorious stories that make up the gospel of God. I call them GodStories.

It's a funny word, and you won't find it in the dictionary. But my guess is that the idea of looking at a gospel through *stories* will excite lots of people. Perhaps you see theology as a rabbit warren of concepts without narratives, a series of points and principles and theories that take all the best bits (like characters and plot twists and heroism) out of the Bible and leave behind a slightly inedible result, like eating cereal without milk or playing Scrabble without vowels. To you, the fact that this book is made up of stories—and, far more importantly, the fact that God's gospel is made up largely of stories—should be encouraging. It will certainly increase your enjoyment of theology.

You see, just as we have one God in three persons and one church made up of many people, so in Scripture we have one gospel made up of many stories. We have one gospel, for sure: a single, unifying, big story about God and creation, man and sin, Jesus and rescue. But we also have many different ways of telling that big story because it is too large for us to grasp all at once. Even the quick summaries in the Bible itself—"your God reigns," "the kingdom of God is near," "God raised Jesus from the dead," and "Christ died for our sins"—give different angles on the one big story. So seeing the many GodStories in the one gospel does not reduce that gospel in glory or splendor. Quite the opposite—it dramatically increases it.

This is true of all sorts of big stories, not just the gospel. Imagine that, instead of writing *The Lord of the Rings*, Tolkien decided to simplify things into a sentence: "Frodo and Sam left the Shire with the ring, faced a number of setbacks, and finally destroyed it in Mount Doom to save Middle-earth." His summary would, in one sense, tell the same story, but it would be dramatically reduced in power and impact, and would probably not have sold millions of copies and been turned into three blockbuster films. *The Lord of the Rings* is about two hobbits and a ring, but it is also about the flight of the elves, the destruction of the forests, the corruption of humankind, the battles for Rohan and Gondor, the return of the king, and the influence the ring has on all of them. So when we read all those other stories, it adds to our understanding of the plot with Frodo and the ring, because it shows us the significance of the main story through its impact on all the others. The same is true of the gospel. But the process is far more important, for three reasons.

GodStories and the Glory of God

The first and biggest reason we must read these stories is because the glory of God is at stake. This is vital. If the Bible is stuffed full of GodStories but we tell only one of them, we lose much of the depth and wonder of the gospel, and that diminishes our view of God, just as it would diminish my view of Gordon Ramsay's cooking if I ate only his steamed vegetables.

If, for example, we saw the gospel simply as a story of personal salvation, we would limit its scope enormously and rob God of the praise that is due to him. Such a view would miss out on the salvation of a corporate people and would find very little place for the history of Israel, which so much of the Bible is about. It would marginalize God's faithfulness to his covenant and his multicolored wisdom in the church. And it would ignore the fact that Scripture speaks of the whole of creation, not just human souls, being made new. So reducing the gospel to only a story of personal salvation is like playing "Bohemian Rhapsody" on the recorder. The melody might be the same, but much of the music's power is lost, and the brilliance of the composer is missed.

Yet, as with music, God's excellence is shown not just in creating new story lines, but in fusing them together so that they enhance one another. Queen brings two melodies together to form a harmony, but Yahweh weaves dozens of GodStories—Abraham, Jacob, Joseph, Moses, David, and many others—into one another so intricately that when Jesus finally arrives on the scene, you want to stand amazed and applaud with excitement. Composers frequently write notes that clash with one another to present an unusual sound, but God allows entire plotlines to clash for generations and then get explained with a twist you would never have predicted (a servant king, for instance). Queen leaves their final chord sequence unresolved for several seconds, but God leaves Psalm 22 and Isaiah 53 unresolved for several centuries before uniting them at the cross with unimaginable power and beauty. So to grasp more of the glory of God, we need to appreciate the range and depth of the gospel by studying as many of its component stories as possible. More than anything else, the reason for writing a book full of GodStories is to remind us how astonishing and faithful and glorious and worthy of worship is the God who wrote them.

This could not be more important. If God's glory is infinite, and my concept of him is not, then I never stop needing an increased understanding of his greatness. Furthermore, that greatness is many-sided, like a massive mountain; there is nowhere in creation I could stand and see the whole of Mount Kilimanjaro at once, far less the glory of Yahweh. So I need there to be a whole host of pictures to reveal different angles of what he has done and how it fits together. Fortunately, by his grace, this is exactly the sort of Bible he has inspired.

Scripture contains something to inspire worship in everyone. To the philosopher, there are GodStories of riddles and revelation, inquiry and truth. To the historian, there is an array of events covering thousands of years and numerous civilizations. To the architect, there are descriptions of temples being established and cities being rebuilt. To the artist, there are GodStories of beauty triumphing over ugliness, order over chaos, new creation over stagnation. For the romantic, there is a tale of a complicated relationship with a wonderful man that ends happily ever after; for the action-film fanatic, a story of a hero rescuing the love of his life and saving the world against impossible odds.[2] There are genealogies for the tribesmen, visions for the mystics, and arguments for the intellectuals. And displaying his glory in every one of these GodStories is Yahweh, the I AM, the maker of heaven and earth and the rescuer of all things. Reading all of these stories will give us a bigger and better view of him.

GodStories and the Rescue of People

The second reason that we need to know these GodStories is because people's eternal destinies are at stake. After all, the gospel is "the power of God for salvation to everyone who believes" (Rom. 1:16), and preaching the gospel remains one of the highest callings of every Christian. Without the gospel, people cannot be saved. So it is vital that we know what the gospel actually is and how to communicate it in ways people understand.

Everyone agrees with that sentence, I'm sure. But read it again, because it is more difficult than it sounds: It is vital to know what the gospel is and how to communicate it in ways people understand. Many churches are great at half of this but neglect the other half. Some churches know the gospel inside out but put a lot of religious or cultural baggage on it, and are therefore not very effective at communicating it to a pluralist and largely pagan culture. On the other hand, there are churches who have gotten very good at using culture to communicate the gospel but have in the process lost sight of what they were supposed to be communicating. To be effective missionaries to our culture, we need to have fixed theology and flexible culture—strong on what the gospel is, but communicating it without adding religious clutter to it—or, more eloquently, "reaching out without selling out."[3]

Paul is a great model. No one could accuse Paul of not knowing the gospel or of being scared to preach it. The scars on his back and welts on his face from being stoned and flogged would see to that. Yet he used a wide range of GodStories to communicate the gospel, depending on his setting.

To the Jews in Damascus, he proved that Jesus was the Messiah (Acts 9:22). To the Jews in Pisidian Antioch, he preached forgiveness of sins and freedom from the law through Jesus' resurrection (Acts 13:16–41). To the pagans in Lystra, he spoke of the creator God who showed his presence by giving them crops and good weather (Acts 14:14–17). To the pagans in Athens, he proclaimed an independent God who did not need serving and who would one day judge the world (Acts 17:22–31). To King Agrippa and Festus, he shared his personal testimony (Acts 26:1–23). So, although we know from Romans that Paul was utterly convinced of justification by faith, redemption, and being in Christ, we know from Acts that these weren't always the GodStories he started with or stuck to when preaching to unbelievers. Others, equally true, were often more appropriate to his audience.

In none of this are we saying the gospel needs to change. That would be a terrible mistake because it puts the desires of man above the desires of God, which is idolatry. What we are saying is that there are numerous GodStories in Scripture, and it might be that the best way of saving some of God's image-bearers is to start our preaching with a slightly different GodStory than the ones we are used to. The main planks of the gospel—a loving God, fallen humanity, rescue through the death and resurrection of Jesus, and so on—will never alter. But how we nail the planks together might.

GodStories and the Health of the Church

The third and final reason for writing *GodStories* is partly a product of the first two: The health of the church is on the line. At one level, this is obvious: If the church isn't worshipping God properly or reaching the world with the gospel, then it is a waste of space and time. There is more to it than that, however. Again and again in the pages of the New Testament, we find writers contending for the gospel because they care about the church.

To the Galatians, Paul reinforces GodStories about being justified by faith apart from the law, and about Jews and Gentiles being one in Christ.[4] The Corinthians, on the other hand, seem to understand that, but need a strong reminder about Christ being crucified, their sanctification, and the bodily resurrection. First John focuses on the incarnation GodStory more than others. Hebrews tells us about the priesthood of Jesus and the superiority of Christ to the major Jewish symbols. In none of these cases is evangelism the point. Instead, a failure to understand these various GodStories leads to division and sexual immorality and false teaching and backsliding, respectively. So the health of the church depends on understanding the fullness of the gospel.

The gospel is not just for guest meetings or open airs, as you would think to hear us sometimes, but for the people of God. The outstanding explanation of the gospel in Romans, remember, was written to Christians; Paul tells Timothy to preach the word to his church until he's blue in the face (2 Tim. 4:2); and Paul's aim to visit the capital of the world was generated by a desire to preach the gospel among the church there (Rom. 1:15). If preaching the gospel to the church means simply reiterating the call to repent and be saved every week, then it is no wonder that so many preachers (and listeners) struggle. But if it means explaining to the church the full extent and scope of the GodStories in Scripture, then you could preach for a lifetime and never repeat yourself.

Thank God that there are so many to go round. If you're in an introverted community of mature Christians, you can study the mission of God. If you love seeing people saved but you aren't quite sure what to do with them when they are, you can look at freedom from sin. Frustrated artists can look at God's beauty; frustrated activists, his justice. If you don't get the Old Testament, then you can look under every verse and every rock until you find Christ. If you get only the Old Testament, then see how all of God's promises are now *yes* and *amen*. Whoever you are, wherever you're reading this, you can find a GodStory that will expand your view of God and revel in it. Then you can experience the joy of sharing it, in a culturally appropriate way, with someone who doesn't know it yet. The world has nothing in comparison.

So we need to know and preach and live the gospel. The good news that shines through all the GodStories will bring us closer into worship, push us further into mission, and draw us closer into community— facedown, flat out, all in. This book is just an introduction to a few of them. But they might change your life all the same.

GodStories usually do.

Endnotes

1. The names of the people in this story have been changed.

2. Adapted from David Murrow, *Why Men Hate Going to Church* (Nashville, TN: Nelson, 2005), 15.

3. This phrase is the subtitle of Mark Driscoll's excellent book on the subject, *The Radical Reformission* (Grand Rapids, MI: Zondervan, 2004).

4. If, that is, we recognize that Galatians might tell more than one GodStory at once, rather than (as sometimes happens) playing them off against each other. For an excellent explanation of how we can and should embrace both these GodStories together, see Stephen Westerholm, *Perspectives Old and New on Paul: The "Lutheran" Paul and His Critics* (Grand Rapids, MI: Eerdmans, 2004).

ACT ONE
CREATION AND FALL

CREATION THROUGH CHRIST

*For by him all things were created, in heaven
and on earth, visible and invisible, whether
thrones or dominions or rulers or authorities—
all things were created through him and for
him. And he is before all things, and in him all
things hold together. —Colossians 1:16–17*

Creation tells us GodStories every day, if only we have eyes to look for them. The heavens tell us about glory, the stars about sustaining power, the sun and moon about God's otherness than us. Human bodies tell us about how careful and wonderful God's design is, and numerous creatures display his wisdom. From the moment Genesis announces "In the beginning, God created ..." there is a GodStory, even though we do not hear about human beings for another twenty-six verses. It's a GodStory about the supremacy of the One by whom and for whom everything was created, and in whom all things hold together.

Studying the size of the heavens, as David and Isaiah urge us to, leads us to consider the incomparable size and power of almighty God. It's well worth doing.[1] But in this narrative, we're going to do the opposite of that. We're going to study some of the smaller things in creation to see if we can get more insight into the One who created them.

Start with Earth. Relative to space, Earth is pretty small. The northern lights on Jupiter, which is a tiny fraction of the size of any star, are bigger than our entire planet. But relative to Earth, everything we might otherwise think of as huge is actually tiny. We tend to think of mountains and ocean trenches as being enormous—giant ridges on Earth's surface that must mean the planet is shaped like an old cannonball, with massive bumps and craters everywhere. However, as big as these mountain ranges and ocean trenches are compared to us, they are tiny compared to Earth. In fact, relative to its size, Earth is smoother than a billiard ball, even with the Andes Mountains and the Java Trench.

But on the surface of this rather small planet, all around its relatively small mountain ranges and forests, are billions of creatures which are so tiny that the vast majority of them cannot be seen with the naked eye. In the top inch of forest soil, there are 340 different animals under the area covered by my footprint. That means that when I go for a one-mile walk, I tread on approximately six hundred thousand creatures, none of which I ever see.[2] These animals tell me a GodStory about the care and providence of almighty God. "Are not two sparrows sold for a penny? And not one of them will fall to the ground apart from your Father" (Matt. 10:29).

These tiny creatures are the tip of the iceberg, though. You probably know about cells, for example. Your entire body is made up of them, and there are over one hundred million of them in the human eye alone. Bacteria cells are so minuscule that they carpet your body at all times without you ever realizing; when you wash your hands, you scrub around five million of them off your hands and into the sink.[3] "All things were created … visible and invisible."

It doesn't stop there. Cells are themselves made up of even smaller entities which we have only started to understand quite recently. The intestinal bacterium, which is small for a cell (about 0.0001cm wide), has inside it twenty thousand ribosomes, which are basically miniature chemical factories that produce protein molecules for the cell to use. Molecules are so small that you have to use quite ridiculous analogies to visualize them. For instance, if you placed a water molecule next to an orange, the size difference would be similar to placing a pea next to Earth. Beneath them, molecules are themselves composed of atoms, which are even more unimaginably small. Why and how did God make things as small as that? Because of, and by, the hero of our creation GodStory, Jesus. "All things were created through him and for him."

When you get inside the atom, things become a little bit confusing, since there is a lot of dispute about what is in there. Chemists are agreed on electrons, neutrons, and protons, but there appear to be even smaller particles within each of these, like leptons and quarks (as a frame of reference, a hydrogen atom is reckoned to weigh about two thousand times the mass of a lepton). Whilst these almost infinitesimal particles are being theorized about—we have to theorize, you see, because even with electron microscopes, they are too small for us to see them—there remains huge debate about how they constitute matter at all, and what knits them together. In scientific terms, it's a mystery. But theologically, the answer is simple: "He is before all things, and in him all things hold together."

Creation points to the supremacy of Christ. The heavens declare his glory, the earth his wisdom, the cell his providence, and the lepton his inconceivable attention to detail. And he loves it:

*When [Yahweh] marked out the foundations
of the earth, then I was beside him, like a
master workman ... rejoicing before him always,
rejoicing in his inhabited world and delighting
in the children of man. (Prov. 8:29–31)[4]*

Endnotes

1. Readers eager to grasp the glory of God in the size of creation might be interested to view Mike Gilbert's superb video at www.GodStoriesBook.com.

2. There are an average of 1,356 living creatures in one foot of forest soil, my footprint is about one quarter of one square foot, and one mile is about 1,750 paces. The former statistic is from Annie Dillard, *Pilgrim at Tinker Creek* (New York: Harper's Magazine, 1974), 94.

3. Philip Yancey and Paul Brand, *Fearfully and Wonderfully Made* (Grand Rapids, MI: Zondervan, 1987), 18–19.

4. In Proverbs, of course, this passage is spoken by wisdom, so it might seem strange to attribute it to Jesus. But it is widely accepted that one of the main points of John 1 (not to mention Colossians 1) is that Jesus *is* the wisdom of God, the master workman by whom all things were made.

THE IMAGE OF GOD

*Then God said, "Let us make man in our image,
after our likeness...." So God created man in his own
image, in the image of God he created him; male
and female he created them. —Genesis 1:26-27*

You are the second-most sacred thing in the universe. If someone was to draw up a list of holiness starting with the most holy, God would be at the top, and immediately beneath him would be you and the billions of other people who have been made in God's image over the last six thousand years. Not lions, cows, or toucans. Not mountains, stars, or supernovas. People. You and I are completely unlike the rest of creation. We are made in the image of God.

That has lots of implications. It has implications for war and justice and abortion and sex trafficking. It has implications for worship and church and mission and art. The fact that we rarely think about those implications does not mean they aren't there. It may simply mean that we have not really grasped how utterly radical Genesis 1:27 actually is.

The most obvious thing "in his own image" means is that we *resemble* God physically. That might sound shocking to some (and sound very obvious to others), but it's the truth: We look like God. That is what the words *image* and *likeness* normally mean. Sometimes we think that Jesus looked like us because he was God in *our* image. But that's back to front. We look like we do because we are made in *his* image. When God takes flesh—whether as Jesus, or as the angel of Yahweh, or the commander of Yahweh's army, or whatever—he doesn't look like a lion, a cow, or a toucan, but a human being, complete with large brain and vertical spine and opposable thumbs.

It is not just our bodies that are in God's image. We also have the capacity to *reason* like God, in a way quite distinct from the rest of the animal kingdom. Sure, some animals can learn from experience and solve problems, but the faculty of abstract reasoning, best demonstrated in our use of language, is uniquely human. Consider a small child learning English. The child catches a ball and shouts with delight, "I catched it!" She is not repeating something, because she has never heard that word in her life. Instead, she has linked together two abstract ideas—the verb *catch* and the past tense *-ed*—and combined them in a way she has never observed. That capacity to reason is uniquely human and is a product of being made in the image of a reasoning, thinking God.

Now move on to the next clause: "Male and female he created them." God created both men and women in his image so that they could *relate* like God. Because God is three in one, he lives in community and relationship, so the creatures in his image do as well. That's why God said it was a bad idea for us to be alone: We are made for relationship with other people, and without it we cannot cope (which is why solitary confinement in prison is such a severe punishment). Note also that both men and women are equally created in the image of God. Again, this may seem obvious to us today, in a world that has been shaped by biblical values for hundreds of years, but it was extremely radical when Scripture was written, and it still is in much of the world. Even Plato thought that women were reincarnated men who had lived poor lives, and Aristotle, another great philosopher, maintained that women were mutilated men produced by inadequate fathers. But Scripture is emphatic: Humans are made for relationship, and both men and women are God's image.

If you read verse 28, you'll see that there are two more aspects to being in God's image, one of which is *reproducing* like God. Just as God loves to create new things and to make creatures that are just like him, so we have a desire to do the same. The last one is even clearer, and is arguably the main point of the entire passage: Being made in God's image means *ruling* like God. We are like God, and God rules over all things, so it is only natural that he should delegate *us*, not lions or cows or toucans, to govern his world. Which he does: "Fill the earth," "subdue it," "have dominion over every living thing." That is part of what being created in God's image means.

So that's what the image of God is all about. And this is actually where most GodStories start. God, as we read frequently in Scripture, wanted his glory to fill the whole earth, so he made human beings in his image—creatures who resembled, reasoned, related, reproduced, and ruled like him—and told them to fill the earth. But they spoiled the image of God through sin. Every aspect of the image of God in humanity, from physical well-being to mental processes to relationships to sex to good government, was distorted at the fall. So God set about the restoration of his image in people, his recovery of the way they had originally been created, so that his glory could truly fill the whole earth. In this sense, the rest of the Bible—Abraham,

Moses, Israel, even Jesus—are part of this GodStory, the restoration of the image of God in humans.

This restoration is important, because when people see you, they form conclusions about God. That's why people with abusive fathers find it so hard to conceive of God properly; people were intended to carry the image of God, to show the world what God is like. We were never identical to God, of course, for that honor is reserved for Jesus. But we stand to God rather like a photograph does to a person: It may be two-dimensional, and much smaller, but it's the best way of showing what someone is like if they are not there.

So you're part of the most exciting project going on today: the restoration of the image of God in humanity. As a human being, you have value not just for what you do, but for who you are, and ultimately for who you represent—and so do the thirteen hundred people who have been born while you read this narrative. We all bear the image of God.

THE BLUEPRINT

And God blessed them. And God said to them, "Be
fruitful and multiply and fill the earth and subdue
it and have dominion over the fish of the sea and
over the birds of the heavens and over every living
thing that moves on the earth." —Genesis 1:28

Quick question: What's the first thing God ever tells humankind to do in Scripture? Hint: It has nothing to do with avoiding apples, and if you skipped the Bible verse above, you skipped the answer. The first thing God gives man is a blessing, not a ban, with profoundly exciting and fulfilling implications. In essence: Have sex, have babies, travel, explore, and take charge over all you see.

Most people I know are quite into all those things, but it can come as a surprise to discover that God put those desires there in the first place. He created us with the desire to be fruitful, multiply, fill the earth, and subdue it. He invented the desire to travel, control our environment, have families, and have sex (and if you don't believe me, read through Genesis and the Song of Songs). Not only did he invent those desires, he actively encouraged us to fulfill them, and they form his blueprint for human beings.

We saw in the last narrative that there was a very good reason for this blueprint. God wanted to fill the earth with his glory, so he made a creature that would bear his image and glory and then told that creature to fill the earth. The idea was, as they had sex and had babies and went to the ends of the earth, there would be billions of them, and they would take the image and glory of God with them to Patagonia and Kamchatka and Irian Jaya and Mauritania. In this way, the earth would be filled with the glory of Yahweh, just like the waters fill the sea.

Well, skeptics might say, that plan blew up in his face. The image of God was spoiled through sin, and man started deliberately undermining every aspect of his magnificent blueprint—abusing sex, trashing the earth, killing each other, and building cities to avoid spreading out. But that reading of events fails to see the wisdom of God. He let man's foolishness run its course for a while, and then set about restoring the blueprint, through an idol-worshipping pagan named Abram. In several installments starting in Genesis 12, Yahweh blessed Abram, told him he would be exceptionally fruitful, promised him uncountable children, renamed him Abraham, and said he would father many nations and bless the world. The idea was, as Abraham and his offspring had sex and babies, there would be billions of them, and they would take the image and glory of God with them to Patagonia and Kamchatka and Irian Jaya and Mauritania. Within a few hundred years, sure enough:

> *But the people of Israel were fruitful and increased greatly; they multiplied and grew exceedingly strong, so that the land [or, the earth] was filled with them. (Ex. 1:7)*

Not that it was plain sailing from this point on. Israel, like the rest of humanity, frequently lived with complete disregard for their blueprint. As the Old Testament story developed, however, rumors began circulating that the blueprint might be in for another restoration. Jewish prophets like Isaiah talked about a way of somehow possessing nations, and of being fruitful and multiplying, without having any physical offspring.[1] No one knew quite what that meant yet, but it sounded like the image and glory of God might reach the nations without the Jews having to conquer them. Mysterious.

Seven hundred years later, another Jewish prophet called Jesus of Nazareth brought the solution to the mystery. He had never had children or even been outside Israel as an adult, but he stood there on a mountain in Galilee and reminded his followers of God's blueprint for humanity—to cover the earth with his glory by filling it with creatures bearing his image:

> Go therefore and make disciples of all nations, baptizing them in the name of the Father and of the Son and of the Holy Spirit, teaching them to observe all that I have commanded you. (Matt. 28:19–20)

Do you see? The blueprint hasn't changed! God is still passionately committed to seeing people carry the image and glory of God. But the blueprint is no longer just about having children (although it will include that for many people); it's about going to the children that are there already and baptizing and teaching them. It is no longer just about filling the spaces where nobody lives; it's about filling the spaces where *everybody* lives with disciples of Jesus. In other words, the blueprint is still for human beings to reproduce themselves and travel. It's just that reproducing yourself is now called discipleship, and travel is now called world mission.

God designed you well. So, whether we're having sex or training children or making disciples or going to unreached people, let's do it with thankfulness to the God of the blueprint. And let's do it with the same passion God has: to see the earth covered with his image and glory, as the waters cover the sea.

Endnote

1. See Isaiah 54:1–5 (barren women) and 56:3–7 (infertile men).

God's blueprint for you is that you make disciples of all nations, whether you go across the world or across the street. And one way of developing a passion for mission is to read the stories of those missionaries who have gone before you.

There are countless books describing the exploits of men and women who lived by God's blueprint and changed the world, one person at a time. Here is a small selection that may help get you started:

- *Hudson Taylor and Maria* by John Pollock
  This story of Hudson Taylor's missionary journey to inland China is one of the classic missionary biographies. His approach fundamentally changed the way that missionary activity worked, and this is a compelling account of it.

- *George Whitefield*, two volumes by Arnold Dallimore
  George Whitefield was one of the finest preachers in history, preaching thirty thousand sermons, and God brought revival to Great Britain through him in the eighteenth century. Dallimore's two-volume treatment is widely recognized as the best on this amazing servant of God.

- *A Chance to Die: The Life and Legacy of Amy Carmichael* by Elisabeth Elliot

  The Irish missionary Amy Carmichael worked in India for fifty-five years, preaching the gospel in word and action. Elisabeth Elliot, whose husband was killed on the mission field, tells the story with passion.

- *Blood and Fire: William and Catherine Booth and Their Salvation Army* by Roy Hattersley

  Few people have had as much impact in Britain as William and Catherine Booth, founders of the Salvation Army. This biography, by a non-Christian historian and politician, is an excellent portrayal of how they did it.

- "You Will Be Eaten by Cannibals! Lessons from the Life of John G. Paton" by John Piper, available at www. DesiringGod.org/ResourceLibrary/Biographies/

  John Piper's outstanding Web site has a number of sketches of people who lived and died by their blueprint. This one, of the South Sea Islands missionary John G. Paton (who famously said it didn't matter whether he was eaten by cannibals or by worms), is very challenging.

GOD AND THE WALK

*And they heard the sound of Yahweh God walking
in the garden in the cool of the day. —Genesis 3:8*

I once heard it said that before judging anybody, you should first walk a mile in their shoes. It makes sense. Not only will you then have an understanding of everything they have been through before you judge them, but you will also be a mile away from them. And you will have their shoes.

We are probably familiar with the notion that Jesus walked a mile in our shoes. What we may not realize is that the whole Bible, from Genesis to Revelation, is the GodStory of a personal God who walks among his people. Theologians call this *immanence*, which is the idea that God is present among us, and it is deeply radical. Try telling a devout Muslim that you believe God walks among his people, and you'll get a sense of how radical. But Scripture puts the immanence of the walking God slap bang in the center.

The walk starts in the garden. It was hot in the middle of the day, so Adam and Eve would have remained in the shade, but in the late afternoon and early evening they would go for a walk, and Yahweh would walk with them. In our sin-tainted world it is hard to imagine what that might be like, but the language of walking suggests a wonderful level of intimacy and closeness, and even informality.

With no sin, there was no barrier between Yahweh and man, no need for sacrifices to overcome the separation between God and the creatures in his image. I wonder what they talked about.

Sadly, this state of affairs did not last forever, because on one of Yahweh's daily walks in the cool of the day, his image-bearers were not waiting for him, but hiding from him. In the judgment that followed, people were banned from returning to the garden, which meant that walking with God became off-limits. But not for long. People soon realized their mistake and started calling on the name of Yahweh, and within a few generations the God of the walk was back, hiking with Enoch and eventually taking him. Then there was Noah, who also walked with God, followed by Abraham, who had the angel of Yahweh walk up to his tent and have lunch. Despite sin, God still loved people, so he walked with them.

You might think that changed with the law of Moses. All those sacrifices and commandments and curtains look like they have separated man from God altogether, and it certainly doesn't look like he's walking among people. But that is exactly what he is doing: "Yahweh your God walks in the midst of your camp" (Deut. 23:14). The law of Moses is a set of instructions about how man should respond to the God of the walk, not evidence that he is no longer there.

Of course, God is spirit and doesn't have a body, so we shouldn't take these passages to mean that there was a massive physical being clomping around campsites in the Middle East. On the other hand, there is a wonderful passage in Daniel that protects us from making the opposite mistake, dialing down the language of "walking" so much that the note of immanent presence is lost. Take a look:

*Then King Nebuchadnezzar was astonished and
rose up in haste. He declared to his counselors,
"Did we not cast three men bound into the fire?"
They answered and said to the king, "True, O
king." He answered and said, "But I see four men
unbound, walking in the midst of the fire, and
they are not hurt; and the appearance of the
fourth is like a son of the gods." (Dan. 3:24–25)*

I think this is why there are so many angels in Scripture. They serve as a regular reminder that, though God is high above, he is still the God of the walk.

With that in mind, consider Jesus. There's nothing metaphorical here: Jesus literally walked many thousands of miles in humanity's shoes. In the first few months of his ministry, Luke records him walking from Nazareth to Judea to Nazareth to Capernaum to Judea to Lake Galilee to Capernaum to Nain, a distance of around 750 miles, and that's without including "going through their towns and cities" and "withdrawing to desolate places." He walked up arid hills and through barren scrubland and down narrow lanes and even on water. He walked with rich and poor, famous and infamous, with no bodyguards or protective cordon, sometimes alone, sometimes through streets so crowded he could hardly move. He walked up the mountain to be transfigured before Moses and Elijah, and then walked down again to be rejected by a Samaritan village so small we don't even know its name. He wore sandals and got blisters and stepped in dung and got physically exhausted. He walked to Golgotha with a wooden stake on his back, then walked out of the tomb and walked to Emmaus. Finally, after walking out to Bethany, he ascended into heaven, walked through the holy places to the right hand of the Father, and with his mission accomplished … he sat down.

But he's still the God of the walk. So as soon as he had finished, he got right up and went for a walk among what Revelation calls "the golden lampstands": his churches. Unlike his earthly walk, this was not a purposeful stride but a gentle amble, a walk of friendship and fellowship, more like Eden than Galilee. After his ascension, he sent his Spirit so that we could have the God of the walk with us at all times, so we could walk in him, keep in step with him, experience his immanent presence with us wherever we are.

God is a God who walks. He sent a Spirit who walks. And in Jesus, he walked a mile in our shoes so we could walk in his.

SHAME REMOVED

And Yahweh God made for Adam and for his wife garments of skins and clothed them. —Genesis 3:21

I don't know whether you've ever had the naked dream—apparently most people have. It's awful. You are in a public place of some sort— an office or (worse) a school—and you gradually become aware of people looking at you and pointing. You try to ignore it, but eventually are forced to look at yourself, and you discover that you are totally naked. In the hallway. The sense of shame and horror is so overwhelming that you usually wake up immediately, shuddering and breathing deeply.

No doubt psychologists have their theories about where the naked dream comes from, but it actually goes back to Eden. It was in Eden that nakedness first became associated with that terrible phenomenon, shame. The story is so well known that we can miss it, but nakedness and shame are intertwined throughout Genesis 2—3, and they have been ever since. The parts of the body that can be displayed publicly vary enormously from culture to culture (just the eyes for Yemeni women, arms and legs in European cities, everything but the genitals in some equatorial tribes), but complete nakedness is rarely normal among adults in public. Somewhere in the human psyche is a primal association between being naked and being ashamed.

To understand this, we need to follow the story of Adam and Eve. When Eve was first brought to Adam, they "were both naked and were not ashamed" (2:25). God had made them without clothes, he had brought them together in the Bible's first marriage, and they were sexually united as one flesh; there was nothing to hide, either physically or spiritually.

But then sin happened. By twisting and misrepresenting God's words, the serpent got the woman, and then the man, to disobey God. We, reading the story thousands of years later, know the consequences: organic sin in the human race, relationship with God broken, perfect creation spoiled, gender roles distorted, and death itself entering the story. But if you read the story carefully, what was the first thing that happened? It might surprise you:

> Then the eyes of both were opened, and they knew that they were naked. And they sewed fig leaves together and made themselves loincloths. (Gen. 3:7)

The first consequence of sin, at least from humankind's point of view, was the shame of nakedness. As if to symbolize the terrible spiritual shame they felt for having broken God's commandment, the man and the woman felt a terrible physical shame for being unclothed. In seconds, Adam and Eve had become sinful creatures before an all-knowing and all-powerful God, and their first instinct (as in all cover-ups from Eden to Watergate) was to conceal everything, including their physical bodies. And so we end up with the bizarre fact that the first action humankind took, on fracturing relationship with Yahweh and introducing death to the human race, was a cringeworthy attempt to make loincloths out of fig leaves to hide their embarrassment. Their second action, trying to hide from God, was similarly motivated, and similarly futile. Nakedness and transparency, intended as blessings, had become a disgrace through the corrupting power of sin.

But there is one thing in the world that can overcome disgrace, and that is grace. Humankind's sin is judged and punished, of course (3:16–19). But whereas humans first response was to hide their nakedness clumsily, God's first action was to hide their nakedness perfectly. Yahweh kills an animal, makes them "garments of skins" from it, and clothes them, removing the crippling dishonor they felt in their nakedness, and demonstrating that even though they were incapable of covering their shame, the living God was not.

Do you see? When confronted with the presence of Yahweh, sin led to an unbearable sense of exposure and humiliation for the man and the woman. And it always does. Human attempts to cope with sin's stigma were futile, and they always have been. It took the gracious intervention of God through a blood sacrifice to remove their disgrace. And it always has.

That day saw a lot of things, but one that gets very little attention is the way God removed the shame of humankind. Their dishonor before God and each other was completely removed. Nakedness, far more humiliating than anything we might feel during the naked dream, was exchanged for clothing. Striving was replaced by sacrifice, shame by shelter, disgrace by grace. So when Scripture speaks of being clothed in garments of salvation (Isa. 61:10), pure vestments (Zech. 3:4), and white linen (Rev. 19:7–8, 14), it is not just telling us of sins forgiven, as wonderful as that is. It is telling us of shame removed.

AUTHORITY REGAINED

And Jesus came and said to them, "All authority in heaven and on earth has been given to me. Go therefore and make disciples of all nations, baptizing them in the name of the Father and of the Son and of the Holy Spirit, teaching them to observe all that I have commanded you." —Matthew 28:18-20

History is about authority. It is about other things as well, but it is always about that. God's story begins and ends with authority being given: God, to the man, to the woman, to Satan, who kept it for a while but was then forced to give it to Jesus, who now holds it and allows men and women to share it, but will one day give it back to God the Father. Eden and Calvary both were battlegrounds of authority, and so are the minds and hearts of every person since. Whether they realize it or not.

Start at the beginning. God's first commandment to man was that he should exercise authority over creation:

Be fruitful and multiply and fill the earth and subdue it and have dominion over the fish of the sea and over the birds of the heavens and over every living thing that moves on the earth. (Gen. 1:28)

This is quite a dramatic piece of delegation! God, who has all authority everywhere and has spent the rest of the chapter speaking space and spiders and sperm whales into being, has given his image-bearers the responsibility of ruling over creation on his behalf. The reason this is surprising is that the way in which humankind goes on to handle this authority will affect the fruitfulness and productivity of the entire universe: just as America flourished under Franklin Roosevelt and Zimbabwe starved under Robert Mugabe, so the fate of Earth is in the hands of its delegated rulers, Adam and Eve. Yet God sees dominion over creation as an integral part of his plan for humankind, so he hands it down. And he waits.

Unfortunately, in Genesis humankind proceeds to exercise authority more like Mugabe than Roosevelt. The man—the head of the relationship, who was created first, named his wife, and was held ultimately accountable for what happened—abdicates his responsibilities by allowing the serpent to tempt his wife, even though he was "with her" at the time (Gen. 3:6). The woman, in charge by default through her husband's sin, then gives implicit authority to the serpent by listening to it instead of Yahweh. In a few verses, a created order that was supposed to run man à woman à serpent has become serpent à woman à man. The results are tragic but predictable. The land, responding to the bungled authority structure, produces thorns and thistles instead of fruitful abundance, and Satan becomes the acting ruler over the earth: the "prince of the power of the air, the spirit that is now at work in the sons of disobedience" (Eph. 2:2).

Throughout the Old Testament, of course, God remained sovereign, and we should not flatter Satan by exaggerating his authority (look at Job 1—2, for instance). But in some ways, Satan continued to hold sway over the earth for thousands of years. Because it was man who was originally given the authority to rule and man who lost it, it had to be a man who regained it. And since no man was up to the job, the effective authority over the earth remained with the Devil, sometimes even called "the god of this world."

Until Jesus. A number of things were at stake during his temptation in the wilderness, but perhaps the most significant was authority over the earth. Satan knew that if he could just get Jesus to acknowledge *his* authority instead of God's, then it was game over. So he offered Jesus all the kingdoms of the world and all their glory in exchange for worship. Given that the alternative way for Jesus to regain man's authority—going to the cross—was so horrendous, this must have seemed a tempting compromise. But Jesus stood firm, refusing to change the plan. In that moment, a time bomb was set next to the Devil's authority over humankind. The fuse was set for three years.

Sure enough, right on time, the bomb went off in spectacular fashion. As Jesus prayed in Gethsemane, remained silent in the trial, and was nailed to a cross on Golgotha, the utter authority of God was never compromised: "Not my will, but yours." "Father, glorify your name." "That the Scriptures might be fulfilled." At long last a man had arisen who would take seriously humanity's commission to govern the earth with God's authority, and the Devil's mandate was destroyed instantly. Just as one man had conceded authority to Satan, one man had wrenched it back. The right to rule creation was now once again in the hands of humankind, through him who is "the head of all rule and authority" (Col. 2:10).

So when Jesus gathered his disciples on a mountain in Galilee and told them "all authority in heaven and on earth has been given to me," he meant it. He had lived a life of unswerving obedience to the will of God, had defied the Devil's temptation at every step, and therefore had regained the authority that had been given to man in the garden. No more would man's dominion be shared with, or even stolen by, other creatures. Jesus, and Jesus alone, would—and did—hold all authority in heaven and on earth.

COFFEE BREAK:

PAUSE AND PRAY
....

It's very easy to think that prayer is about getting God's authority to line up with our decisions. In the greatest of all prayers, however, the focus seems to be more about getting our decisions to line up with God's authority. You might like to pray through this expanded version of the Lord's Prayer, asking God that your life would increasingly reflect his authority and purposes.

> Our Father in heaven, may your name be made holy. May we, and the people we know, treat you with the respect and awe that you deserve. Please give us a true sense of your majesty and splendor, and may those who don't yet know you come to see the glory of the invisible God in Jesus Christ.
>
> Lord, may your kingdom come, and may your will be done on earth as it is in heaven. May your kingly rule be expressed on the earth, until every person and power submits to your authority as they do in heaven. We are desperate for you to return and to bring your kingdom in its fullness—until you do, help us to live according to your purposes in a world that doesn't.
>
> Give us today our daily bread. Everything good comes from you, Father. We depend on you for all our needs, no matter how big or small, and we ask that you would provide both for us, and for all our brothers and sisters today who are struggling for enough to eat.
>
> Forgive us our sins, as we forgive those who sin against us. Frequently, we have tried to live independent of your authority, and we are sorry,

whether we realized we were doing it or not. Please forgive us. At the same time, we forgive all those who have sinned against us, recognizing that our need for forgiveness is no less than theirs.

And lead us not into temptation, but deliver us from evil. We are so easily tempted to live as if you were not in charge of all things—please protect us from this. May we live and think in a way that glorifies you and shows you to be the pearl of great price, the treasure of our hearts.

For yours is the kingdom, the power, and the glory, forever. Lord, no matter what we see, we know that all things sit under your authority. As we ask you for action, provision, forgiveness, and guidance, we remember that the earth is the Lord's and everything in it. Thank you that you are sovereign over all things! Amen.

THE RAINBOW

*When I bring clouds over the earth and the bow is
seen in the clouds, I will remember my covenant that
is between me and you and every living creature of
all flesh. And the waters shall never again become
a flood to destroy all flesh. When the bow is in the
clouds, I will see it and remember the everlasting
covenant between God and every living creature
of all flesh that is on the earth. —Genesis 9:14–16*

Promises make the world go round. They are called contracts, affirmations, oaths, and vows, but promises are everywhere. Last week in the UK, six thousand marriages began with words like "in the presence of God I make this vow." Two centuries ago in Philadelphia, a nation was established with "we mutually pledge to each other our lives, our fortunes, and our sacred honor." Human interactions would be impossible without promises.

Yet of all the people who make promises every day, only God has never broken one.[1] We say that we'll be there, and we're not; we say "I do," and we don't; we tell people we won't let them down, and we do. But God goes on making promise after promise, century after century. And keeping all of them.

One of his oldest ones is the rainbow. This glorious, mysterious, multicolored arc of refracted light has inspired a thousand sighs and a million playgroup paintings, but its first mention in recorded history was as a guarantee of God's promise. And not just any promise: It was the guarantee of a covenant, a special and one-sided promise that God was making unconditionally, never again to destroy the earth by floods. Given man's track record at this point in the story, this was quite a remarkable commitment on God's part. But even more remarkable is the fact that for four thousand years and counting he has never broken it.

If you look at the story of Noah, you will see that the rainbow, perhaps more than anything else, displays God's grace. Man had sinned, committing murder and violence and polygamy and all sorts of other things, and he had sinned so consistently that God was grieved he had made them in the first place. Genesis 6:5 explains how bleak things were, saying, "Every intention of the thoughts of [man's] heart was only evil continually." If ever there was a generation that deserved to get humanity wiped out forever, it was this one: *every* intention, *only* evil, *continually.*

Yet God's response, as so often, is one of unmerited kindness; he destroys the wicked, as befits his justice, but slips several grace-moments into the story. First, he rescues Noah and his family. Then, as soon as they leave the ark, he announces that he will never again strike the earth and everything that lives on it (8:21). Next, he reissues the commission he gave to Adam and Eve (9:1), showing that humanity had been given a fresh start and could begin to fill the earth once again as if nothing had happened. Finally, he makes a covenant with Noah for all future generations, giving the rainbow as his sign. From this point on, no matter what man does, God has covenanted not to flood the planet, and the rainbow serves as a permanent reminder.

You see, this covenant is not a contract. A contract is a conditional arrangement: If you give me this, I'll give you that. Generally, if one party breaks a contract, then the other is released from their obligations: "He didn't provide the paint job I wanted, so I don't have to pay him." But the rainbow-covenant is one of grace and is completely one-sided. God covenants never again to destroy humankind for our wickedness, but this is grounded not in our commitment to be righteous, but in his commitment to be gracious. In fact, God knew that man would continue to be wicked, and he made the covenant anyway. He foresaw child sacrifice and child slavery, the Holocaust and the Gulag, adultery and abortion, genocide and rape; but his grace was so extravagant that he guaranteed never to destroy, no matter what happened. He made a completely one-sided covenant and left the rainbow in the sky as a guarantee.

Not only that, but he kept it. This is the second thing the rainbow displays—the faithfulness of God to his covenant. Even the most important promises I have ever made, to my wife, I break on a regular basis; I cannot remember the last day I cherished her as Christ does the church. So when I consider that God made his rainbow-promise four millennia ago and has always kept it exactly, you could say I'm quite impressed.

The rainbow is meant to be beautiful and eye-catching, because it is meant to draw us back to the covenant God made with Noah. Its main purpose in the story, however, is not to remind *us* of God's covenant, but to remind *God*. Of course, in a literal sense God never forgets, but the rainbow brings his promises to mind, and whenever he sees it, there is a divine recommitment never again to destroy the earth. Because he said he wouldn't. Because he made a covenant.

So if you are looking for evidence of the grace and faithfulness of God, I can tell you where to find it: in the pot of gold at the end of the rainbow.

Endnote

1. I owe the following piece of phrasing to John Ortberg.

THE CITY AND THE TOWER

*Then they said, "Come, let us build ourselves a city
and a tower with its top in the heavens, and let us
make a name for ourselves, lest we be dispersed
over the face of the whole earth." And Yahweh
came down to see the city and the tower, which
the children of man had built. —Genesis 11:4–5*

Tell a child about the tower of Babel, and they might well conclude that God doesn't like big buildings. If you're not careful, the story can sound like that. Man gets together and builds a big tower; God doesn't like it; so he cancels the project by muddling up languages, and in one fell swoop produces racial conflict and foreign students and Latin lessons. What is all that about?

Read it carefully, however, and the GodStory of Babel is a powerful statement about the sovereignty of God, the sin of man, and the supremacy of Christ. There is a lot more to it than meets the eye. The curse of Babel is overturned in at least three ways, each of which becomes a major biblical theme in itself. As we look at the incident, you might notice some things you had never seen before.

The first is that the famous tower of Babel is only half the story. Humankind actually decides to build a city *and* a tower, the tower to secure fame and the city to avoid being "dispersed over the face of the whole earth"—a deliberate act of defiance against the living

God. Making a name for themselves, rather than for Yahweh, is an act of smugness at best, idolatry at worst. But building a city to avoid being dispersed is just as bad, because they are disobeying the original commission God had given man to go forth and multiply. Yahweh wanted his glory to fill the earth, so he made people in his image and told them to spread out everywhere (Gen. 1:27–28); but man chose his name instead of God's, and security instead of mission. The city and the tower were equally bad.

It's not about buildings. God is passionate about building: His Son was a construction worker, he gave Noah detailed blueprints on how to build the most stable boat imaginable, architectural plans take up numerous chapters in Scripture, and he described the people of God as a beautiful structure (Ezek. 40—48) and a stunning city (Rev. 21), complete with all measurements. So the issue isn't buildings—it's blasphemy. The city and the tower were built to oppose God, and in Babel's case, the tower was probably a *ziggurat*, a step pyramid used as a temple to false gods. So the author cannot restrain his sarcasm when he comments witheringly that "Yahweh came down to see the city and the tower, which the children of man had built." The designer of Mount Everest is unimpressed; he has to peer down from heaven to find out what all the fuss is about. The confusion of language, and the dispersal, soon follow.

As so often in Scripture, however, the rescue plan starts straightaway. God calls a man from the same part of the world, an idol-worshipper whose community had the same habit of building *ziggurats*, and tells him to go to the land he will be shown. His name is Abram. Yahweh's call is a remarkable reversal of Babel—Abram is to leave his land, rather than stay in his city; all the nations, who have only just been separated from one another, will be blessed through him; and rather than making a name for himself, Abram will have his name made great by Yahweh. Ironically, the greatest name is given to him who makes himself nothing, and the greatest city to him who leaves his home and heads off into a strange land. (This may remind you of someone.)

The second great reversal of Babel occurs at Pentecost. The curse of God at Babel had the obvious effect of causing brothers to become foreigners, making people unable to understand each other, dispersing humanity and bringing God's judgment. In Acts 2, the gift of God at Pentecost does the exact opposite, causing foreigners to become brothers, making people able to understand each other, uniting humanity and bringing God's blessing:

> And they were all filled with the Holy Spirit and began
> to speak in other tongues as the Spirit gave them
> utterance. Now there were dwelling in Jerusalem
> Jews, devout men from every nation under heaven.
> And at this sound the multitude came together, and
> they were bewildered, because each one was hearing
> them speak in his own language. (Acts 2:4-6)

Throughout the history of the church, from Corinth to Korea, the gift of speaking in tongues has served this function. I know of several who have preached in Cantonese and Hindi without ever learning the language, and who have seen people converted doing so. Every time that happens, the blessing overcomes the curse, and Babel is undone.

The ultimate undoing of Babel, however, is still in the future. It has begun, through the establishment of a church where there are no racial boundaries (Col. 3:11), but the best is yet to come. There will be a day when the tower and power of Babel will be permanently destroyed, and when no one will want to make a name for themselves or build a city to avoid dispersion. On that day, there will be one name with no rivalry, one people with no racism, one city with no tower, and one cry on the lips of every person from every language and tongue and dialect:

> After this I looked, and behold, a great multitude that no one could number, from every nation, from all tribes and peoples and languages, standing before the throne and before the Lamb, clothed in white robes, with palm branches in their hands, and crying out with a loud voice, "Salvation belongs to our God who sits on the throne, and to the Lamb!" (Rev. 7:9–10)

ACT TWO
ISRAEL AND HISTORY

THE STORY BENEATH THE STORY

And he said to them, "O foolish ones, and slow
of heart to believe all that the prophets have
spoken! Was it not necessary that the Christ should
suffer these things and enter into his glory?"
And beginning with Moses and all the Prophets,
he interpreted to them in all the Scriptures the
things concerning himself. —Luke 24:25–27

Throughout the Old Testament, there's a story beneath the story. I don't mean a subplot, because that implies a sideshow, a distraction from the main narrative. I mean a story that many of us don't notice, and which you might only understand afterward, but which somehow is the real reason that all the other stories are there. You know the type of story I mean: like when you get to the end of *The Usual Suspects* and realize Kevin Spacey has led you up the garden path, and all the things you've seen in the last two hours need to be completely rethought in the light of that. Or when you discover Brad Pitt and Edward Norton are the same person in *Fight Club*, or that Robert Redford hasn't betrayed Paul Newman after all in *The Sting*. Or when you finish *The Sixth Sense* and find out that Bruce Willis is dead, and you've missed the point of virtually every scene. If a story like this is told well, then when you go through it again, it makes much more sense, and you spot clues everywhere. When you first see it, though, you splutter into your drink in surprise.

With that in mind, consider Emmaus. It's a Sunday afternoon, and two companions, probably a husband and wife, are depressed. Like virtually all first-century Jews, they have spent their whole lives waiting for God to send someone who would deliver Israel from the hands of the Romans, and in the last few months they have come across someone who looks like he fits the bill: a charismatic prophet, mighty in word and deed, called Jesus of Nazareth. In the last few days, however, disaster has struck. Instead of Jesus destroying the Romans, the Romans have destroyed Jesus, and he has been dead for two days. Which means that he can't possibly be Israel's king. The narrative they have been following has ended in tragedy.

At this point, Jesus appears. I don't know about you, but if I had just been resurrected, I would arrive with as much fanfare as possible, maybe falling out of the sky in front of them, and announce, "It's me!" Yet Jesus doesn't do that. In fact, he arrives in such a way that they don't even recognize who he is, and he spends the next hour or two explaining the bombshell, the story beneath the story, the truth that all the Scriptures pointed to even if no one had noticed. It is simply this: "that the Christ should suffer these things and enter into his glory."

The couple on the Emmaus road would not have summarized the Old Testament like that. Neither, presumably, would you. Once you know it, though, it is blindingly obvious. If you reread the Old Testament knowing that there is a story beneath the story—that the Messiah would enter into glory through *suffering*—you notice it in every book. You notice that Genesis is full of altars, where animals that have never done anything wrong are killed on behalf of people, and that it begins and ends with righteous blood being spilt by the wicked. You notice that the rest of the Law is largely comprised of detailed instructions on how people can get made right with God through substitutionary sacrifice (or, put differently, the suffering of the innocent). Then you read Israel's history and find that frequently, those who are faithful to God, like Moses and Samuel and Elijah, are rejected by the people and encounter great suffering for their righteousness. This reaches its pinnacle with King David, who enters his glory and kingship through suffering at the hands of King Saul, then gets rejected by his son and is able to write suffering songs like Psalm 22. When you remember that the Christ was to be the new David, it is hard to escape the conclusion that the Christ would also "suffer these things and enter into his glory."

That's the story beneath the story. It was necessary that the Christ, the anointed one of God for whom the Jews had been waiting for centuries, would suffer death on behalf of his people and then be vindicated. So Jesus, addressing this depressed, disillusioned couple on the Emmaus road, decided not to appear in resplendent glory in front of them, but to take them through a Bible study. He decided to show them that the story of crucifixion and resurrection was exactly what they should expect—and that it was the reason all the other stories (like sacrifice of animals, blood of the innocent, persecution of the righteous, prophecies of the Messiah) were there at all. It worked: "Did not our hearts burn within us while he talked to us on the road, while he opened to us the Scriptures?" (Luke 24:32).

The story beneath the story is just about the most powerful one there is, and not just for worship, but for mission. If you are trying to explain the gospel to a Jew or a Muslim, you may not want to start with the divinity of Jesus or the resurrection, because you will probably be misunderstood. But going back to Abraham and explaining how the whole thing points to the cross, like Jesus does here, might just do the trick. Even if they splutter into their drinks in the process.

COFFEE BREAK:

Just as the prophets pointed forward to Jesus' death on the cross, the Christian church looks back to it. This hymn, written by Samuel Crossman in 1664, is one of the best meditations on the sufferings of Christ you are likely to find. You may want to sing it before sharing communion, remembering what Jesus accomplished through his sacrifice.

> My song is love unknown,
> My Savior's love to me;
> Love to the loveless shown,
> That they might lovely be.
> O who am I, that for my sake
> My Lord should take frail flesh and die?
>
> Sometimes they strew His way,
> And His sweet praises sing;
> Resounding all the day
> Hosannas to their King:
> Then "Crucify!" is all their breath,
> And for His death they thirst and cry.
>
> Why, what hath my Lord done?
> What makes this rage and spite?
> He made the lame to run,
> He gave the blind their sight,
> Sweet injuries! Yet they at these
> Themselves displease, and 'gainst Him rise.
>
> They rise and needs will have
> My dear Lord made away;
> A murderer they saved,
> The Prince of life they slay.

Yet cheerful He to suffering goes,
That He His foes from thence might free.

Here might I stay and sing,
No story so divine;
Never was love, dear King!
Never was grief like Thine.
This is my Friend, in Whose sweet praise
I all my days could gladly spend!

GOD'S MISSION

Then he opened their minds to understand the Scriptures, and said to them, "Thus it is written, that the Christ should suffer and on the third day rise from the dead, and that repentance and forgiveness of sins should be proclaimed in his name to all nations, beginning from Jerusalem." —Luke 24:45-47

God has a mission.[1] It's the biggest mission there is: to fill the earth with his glory by covering it with people who bear his image. It's the oldest mission there is, having been around since humanity started. It's also a dangerous mission, with 171,000 people dying for it every year,[2] and many more being beaten, tortured, imprisoned, or dispossessed. In Luke 24, just after his resurrection, Jesus does a Bible study with his disciples to show them that God's massive, old, and dangerous mission is what the whole Old Testament was about. The mission is this: "That repentance and forgiveness of sins should be proclaimed in his name to all nations, beginning from Jerusalem."

It might not have looked like that to start with. Even the biggest avalanche begins with a small shudder. But that's the mission, and like all good missions, it starts with a problem to be solved. In the first few chapters of Genesis, we encounter the problem of sin and the need for repentance, the reality of judgment, and then in chapter 10 we are introduced to the nations of the world, all seventy of them (remember that number). They're all sinful, and they all need to be forgiven. That's Act One.

Act Two takes a leap across to Ur, in modern-day Iraq, where a completely unremarkable man called Abram is given a completely remarkable promise. "In you," Yahweh says to this pagan from an idol-worshipping city, "all the families of the earth shall be blessed." Fast-forward a bit, and Abraham's grandson Jacob, who was a bit of a scalawag, gets his name changed to Israel and then has twelve sons (remember that number), who form the heads of the twelve tribes of Israel. God's mission to bless the earth has begun.

In the next few centuries, Israel (the nation) gets both a land and a king but doesn't really take its call to be a blessing that seriously, and they end up splitting themselves into two chunks, north (Israel) and south (Judah). As we move into Act Three, where the prophets are the main characters, we find that Israel only sends one—one!—missionary to the nations, and even he is so unhappy about it, he ends up doing time inside a fish to teach him a lesson. At the same time, though, the prophets start getting glimpses of God's promise to bless and teach other nations through them:

> It is too light a thing that you should be my servant to raise up the tribes of Jacob and to bring back the preserved of Israel; I will make you as a light for the nations, that my salvation may reach to the end of the earth. (Isa. 49:6)

When the Old Testament concludes, this still hasn't happened. But the mission of God to bless all the families on earth is still there, hovering in the background.

Cue the lights for Act Four: "The book of the genealogy of Jesus Christ, the son of David, the son of Abraham." With the birth of Jesus, suddenly everything changes. An old saint gives thanks that "a light for revelation to the Gentiles" has been born. Jesus himself gathers and sends a group of twelve, representing Israel, and then a group of seventy, representing the nations of the world (remember those numbers?). He includes people of other nations, healing and teaching them, and then sends out his followers as missionaries to the ends of the earth, to proclaim repentance and forgiveness of sins in all nations. It will start in Jerusalem, he says, but soon you'll be in Judea, Samaria, and even the farthest corners of the world.

And so, in Act Five, the mission of God goes flying out of the blocks. Thousands repent in Jerusalem, Philip preaches in Samaria, Peter sees the Spirit fall on Gentiles, and Paul's team won't stop moving until all the nations have been blessed:

> *Jesus Christ our Lord, through whom we have received grace and apostleship to bring about the obedience of faith for the sake of his name among* all the nations. *(Rom. 1:4-5)*

> *For I tell you that Christ became a servant to the circumcised to show God's truthfulness, in order to confirm the promises given to the patriarchs, and* in order that the Gentiles might glorify God *for his mercy.... And thus I make it my ambition to preach the gospel,* not where Christ has already been named. *(Rom. 15:8-9, 20)*

These people were on fire. They got kicked out of homes and towns, took heavy beatings, were stoned, got shipwrecked, and often got killed. So have millions of God's people since then. Why? Because they have grasped that God's mission was never for his people to sit there and hang out together, or even just to study the Bible and pray together. It was "that repentance and forgiveness of sins should be proclaimed in all nations." That's what drove Abraham, Moses, Isaiah, Jesus, Paul, Phoebe, St. Patrick, John Calvin, William Carey, Hudson Taylor, and Amy Carmichael. It's also what drives every nameless hero who loses career, family, home, or even life to accomplish God's mission. Jim Elliot was right: "He is no fool who gives what he cannot keep to gain that which he cannot lose."[3]

The mission of God will prevail, because Yahweh made a promise to Abraham to bless all the families of the earth, and he's going to keep it. There's still a long way to go, because the best estimates suggest that there are still at least five thousand people groups who have never heard the gospel. But God's mission is advancing. In Nepal in 1960, there were twenty believers; there are now a quarter of a million. In Kyrgyzstan in 1986, there was one believer; there are now four thousand. In AD 30, there were one hundred and twenty on earth who named the name of Christ; there are now about a billion. God's mission is old, and huge, and dangerous, but it's going to succeed.

And unlike some GodStories, it's waiting to be completed. Who's in?

Endnotes

1. I am thankful to David Devenish for much of what follows.

2. International Bulletin of Missionary Research, January 2008.

3. From the diary of Jim Elliot, October 28, 1949. Elliot was a missionary to the Auca Indians in Ecuador, and he was hacked to death with wooden machetes for preaching the gospel on January 8, 1956.

MOUNT MORIAH

[God] said, "Take your son, your only son Isaac,
whom you love, and go to the land of Moriah, and
offer him there as a burnt offering on one of the
mountains of which I shall tell you." —Genesis 22:2

The history of God's people begins and ends with fathers being willing to sacrifice their sons. In both sons lay the hope of the world; in both fathers, a love beyond reason.

It is the middle of the night when a 110-year-old man hears the voice of God. Abraham has heard this voice before. The voice told him to leave his land and start traveling with no map and no destination, so he did. It had told him he would have billions of descendants but needed to chop some animals in half and then circumcise both himself, at age ninety-nine, and his teenage son (probably with flint knives), so he did. It then told him to trust that his ninety-year-old wife would have a baby, so—with a bit of encouragement from some visiting angels—he did. But now, the voice is telling him to sacrifice the son through whom God would fulfill his promise of a massive family and inheritance, for which Abraham originally left his home and cut off his foreskin. I suspect there was a moment's hesitation.

But Abraham's track record of hearing and obeying the voice

had set him in good stead, and he trusts his God. So early in the morning, he wakes his son, takes a couple of servants, and heads off for a three-day hike to Mount Moriah. His lack of an animal makes Isaac curious, but Abraham only reminds him of God's provision. As he ties his son down to the altar, imagine the doubts that must have flooded his mind: *What about God's promise to bless the world through my children? Has he changed his mind? Have I upset him? Is Yahweh a covenant-breaker, or perhaps a manipulative tyrant? Did I simply imagine he was telling me to do this?* Yet in disciplined faith, learned from a lifetime of trusting obedience, Abraham raises the knife and prepares to plunge it into the love of his life and the hope of the nations. It is then, and only then, that God tells Abraham not to harm the boy and provides a replacement sacrifice for him.

Frequently, we stop the story there. We celebrate the faithfulness of God and his revelation as Yahweh-will-provide, we think about the ram who acts as a substitute for Isaac, or we marvel at Abraham's faith, seeing in him an example for our own lives (like, for instance, James 2:20–24 and Hebrews 11:17–19). The result of the story, however, is often missed:

> *And the angel of Yahweh called to Abraham a second time from heaven and said, "By myself I have sworn, declares Yahweh, because you have done this and have not withheld your son, your only son, I will surely bless you, and I will surely multiply your offspring as the stars of heaven and as the sand that is on the seashore." (Gen. 22:15-17)*

Do you see? The outcome of the narrative is that Yahweh, with his eyes fixed on the altar, is able to tell Abraham: Now I know for certain that you love me, because you did not spare your own son. I knew you loved me before, but now your faithfulness has been demonstrated once and for all, so I promise I will bless you throughout all generations.

The powerful symbolism of this event shows the degree of control God has over human history. Four millennia later, disciples of Jesus, with our eyes fixed on the cross, can see an offering that shows an even greater love, as the true hope of the nations is killed for all people. So we are able to tell God the Father: Now I know for certain that you love me, because you did not spare your own Son. I knew you loved me before, but now your faithfulness has been demonstrated once and for all. So I promise I will bless your name throughout all generations.[1]

Funnily enough, that's not the last we see of Mount Moriah. About a thousand years later, a prophet called Gad approaches King David and tells him to build a second altar there, in the same place as Abraham's had been, to seek Yahweh's forgiveness for the people (2 Sam. 24:21; 2 Chron. 3:1). It is on this site that Solomon, David's son, later builds the temple of Yahweh in Jerusalem: the place where God meets man, where sacrifice is offered, and where God's forgiveness for the people is found. When God tells Abraham to build an altar to sacrifice "on one of the mountains of which I shall tell you," we don't think much of it. But God knows what he is doing.

And about a thousand years after that, a third altar is established on Mount Moriah, about half a mile from the temple, at a place known locally as the hill of the skull. It is like other altars in many ways—made of wood, a place where God meets man, where sacrifice is offered, and where God's forgiveness for the people is found—but in one respect Moriah's third altar is totally different from the previous two, and from every other altar there has ever been. It is shaped like a cross.

Endnote

1. I owe this way of putting it to Tim Keller, in his talk on "Gospel-Centered Ministry" at the Gospel Coalition conference in 2007.

THE SEED
·················

*Now the promises were spoken to Abraham and
to his seed. He does not say, "And to seeds," as
referring to many, but rather to one, "And to your
seed," that is, Christ. —Galatians 3:16 NASB*

I'm often amazed at the difference one letter can make. Entire
worldviews can change because someone adds a letter where there
wasn't supposed to be one, or drops one when there was. In the
fourth century, some heretics put one letter into a Greek word and
declared Jesus was of a similar substance to the Father (*homoiousios*),
but not the same (*homoousios*), and entire creeds were written to sort
it all out. Atheism and theism are one letter different but complete
opposites. On January 2, 2007, CNN issued a formal apology to a
presidential candidate because of one letter, as footage of a terrorist
manhunt was accompanied with the caption "Where is Obama?"
Similarly, you can imagine a woman's disapproval on being sent a
card by her boyfriend saying "Wish you were her." One letter can be
very important.

It is never more important than in God's promises to Abraham,
though.[1] Paul is adamant about this, as we have just read: The fact
that God made the promises to Abraham's "seed," rather than his
"seeds," suggests that ultimately one person, rather than a group of

people, would fulfill them. The promises to Abraham—which pretty much the whole Bible is about!—are not going to be fulfilled in a random group of descendants, or even in God's chosen nation of Israel, but in one person: Christ.

So what were the promises to Abraham? For that, we need to go back to Genesis:

> *Yahweh appeared to Abram and said, "I will give this land to your seed." (Gen. 12:7 WEB)*

> *I will greatly multiply your seed as the stars of the heavens and as the sand which is on the seashore; and your seed shall possess the gate of their enemies. In your seed all the nations of the earth shall be blessed, because you have obeyed My voice. (Gen. 22:17–18 NASB)*

I count four promises there. One, that the seed will be given the land of Israel; two, that the seed will be incredibly numerous; three, that the seed will have jurisdiction over his enemies; and four, that the seed will be a blessing to all the nations of the earth. Quite a sweeping set of promises, I think you'll agree.

Which makes it very surprising that they are all fulfilled in one person. It sounds strange that it was the "seed," Christ, and not Israel as a whole, that would inherit the land of Israel forever and be incredibly numerous. Yet that is what Paul says. If you think Abraham's promises will be inherited by the whole of ethnic Israel, as lots of people both then and now might tell you, you have misread one crucial letter—it says "seed," not "seeds"—and done the equivalent of writing "wish you were her." Read it carefully, and you'll see that all of these things were to be fulfilled in one person, Jesus Christ.

This is not some new idea that Paul came up with in one of his more eccentric moments. It has always been part of God's plan to focus his promise on one person. Even in Genesis 22, the "seed" cannot mean all of Abraham's descendants, because the promise runs through Isaac and not Ishmael. The next generation, it is narrowed again, to Jacob and not Esau. And so it goes on, getting more specific each time: Judah ahead of his brothers, then the line of Jesse, then David, then Solomon, and finally Christ. God has always wanted to focus all his power and promises through one person.

It was Jesus (the "seed"), and not ethnic Israel (the "seeds"), that would inherit the land of Israel forever, be as numerous as the stars, rule over his enemies, and bless the entire world. This of course raises the questions: In what sense has Jesus been given the land, and in what sense is he "numerous"? For the answer, we need to return to Galatians:

> *For you are all sons of God through faith in Christ Jesus.* For as many of you as were baptized into Christ have put on Christ. *There is neither Jew nor Greek, there is neither slave nor free, there is neither male nor female; for you are all one in Christ Jesus.* And if you are Christ's, then you are Abraham's seed, and heirs according to the promise. *(Gal. 3:26–29 NKJV)*

Can you see what Paul is saying? He is arguing that everyone who was baptized into Christ has "put on" Christ, and somehow been incorporated into him. That means that Abraham's seed, Christ, includes everyone who has been baptized into him. If I put a piece of chewing gum in my mouth and climb Table Mountain, the chewing gum gets to the summit too because it is inside of me, and it is the same with us when we are in Christ. So the land, and in fact the whole earth (Rom. 4:13), are inherited by those who have "put on" Abraham's seed, Christ. And the blessing to all nations comes through those who are in Christ: you, me, Peter, William Wilberforce, Gladys Aylward, Desmond Tutu.

It's not an easy idea, so let's use an analogy. Imagine that in 1840 God promises a Scot named Hugh Fleming that his seed will save millions of lives around the world. Hugh then has eight children, but by the time he dies, none of them have saved anybody. In 1928, however, his seventh child, Alexander, discovers penicillin, which marks the start of modern antibiotics and will end up saving millions of lives. God's promise is true.

Now imagine that the rest of Hugh's children reject Alexander and penicillin. That wouldn't undermine God's promise, would it? It would just show that the way to inherit the promise and save millions of lives would be to join their brother, telling everyone about penicillin and distributing it as far as possible. But—and here's the twist—that option is not only open to Hugh's children, but to anybody else who shows confidence in his discovery. The true heirs of the promise to Hugh are not the natural children who reject his son. The true heirs of the promise are the thousands of doctors and researchers around the world who have faith in penicillin, and do all they can to spread it throughout the world to save people. "If you are Christ's, then you are Abraham's seed, and heirs according to the promise."

You and I, along with the rest of God's global church, are the heirs of the earth. We're the hope of the world. Because of one letter.

Endnote

1. Pedants will object that although there is only one letter's difference between the singular and plural in English, there are more than that in both Greek and Hebrew. But the point stands about crucial differences in meaning turning on slight differences in spelling.

COFFEE BREAK:

If the promises to Abraham are ultimately fulfilled in Christ, rather than in all ethnic Israelites, it makes a lot of difference to our lives. It affects our understanding of Scripture, our prayers, our mission, and even our politics. So it is worth making sure we've understood it properly. Here are a number of texts that teach that everyone in Christ, rather than everyone biologically descended from Abraham, is the true heir of the promises.

> *For circumcision indeed is of value if you obey the law, but if you break the law, your circumcision becomes uncircumcision. So, if a man who is uncircumcised keeps the precepts of the law, will not his uncircumcision be regarded as circumcision? Then he who is physically uncircumcised but keeps the law will condemn you who have the written code and circumcision but break the law. For no one is a Jew who is merely one outwardly, nor is circumcision outward and physical. But a Jew is one inwardly, and circumcision is a matter of the heart, by the Spirit, not by the letter. His praise is not from man but from God. (Rom. 2:25–29)*

> *But it is not as though the word of God has failed. For not all who are descended from Israel belong to Israel, and not all are children of Abraham because they are his offspring, but "Through Isaac shall your offspring be named." This means that it is not the children of the flesh who are the children of God, but the children of the promise are counted as offspring. (Rom. 9:6–8)*

*Therefore remember that at one time you Gentiles in
the flesh, called "the uncircumcision" by what is called
the circumcision, which is made in the flesh by hands—
remember that you were at that time separated from
Christ, alienated from the commonwealth of Israel
and strangers to the covenants of promise, having
no hope and without God in the world. But now in
Christ Jesus you who once were far off have been
brought near by the blood of Christ. For he himself
is our peace, who has made us both one and has
broken down in his flesh the dividing wall of hostility
by abolishing the law of commandments expressed in
ordinances, that he might create in himself one new
man in place of the two, so making peace, and might
reconcile us both to God in one body through the
cross, thereby killing the hostility. And he came and
preached peace to you who were far off and peace
to those who were near. For through him we both
have access in one Spirit to the Father. (Eph. 2:11–18)*

*In Christ Jesus you are all sons of God, through
faith. For as many of you as were baptized into
Christ have put on Christ. There is neither Jew nor
Greek, there is neither slave nor free, there is no
male and female, for you are all one in Christ Jesus.
And if you are Christ's, then you are Abraham's
offspring, heirs according to promise. (Gal. 3:26–29)*

THE PASSOVER

*For I will pass through the land of Egypt that
night, and I will strike all the firstborn in the land of
Egypt, both man and beast; and on all the gods of
Egypt I will execute judgments: I am Yahweh. The
blood shall be a sign for you, on the houses where
you are. And when I see the blood, I will pass over
you, and no plague will befall you to destroy you,
when I strike the land of Egypt. —Exodus 12:12–13*

My father-in-law drives like a maniac. He tears around town in his
red truck, speeding, going the wrong way down one-way streets,
running red lights, cutting off other drivers, and even going around
roundabouts anticlockwise. Yet in twenty years of driving his red
truck, he has never once been stopped or cautioned by the police.
Because his red truck is a fire engine, with a flashing blue light on
top. And the flashing blue light makes all the difference.

Flashing blue lights, passports, PINs, and clubcards are all symbols
of membership that allow you certain privileges, and they allow you
these privileges regardless of your suitability or behavior. People get
into Britain because of their passports, not their knowledge of the
rules of cricket. ATMs give me cash because of my PIN, not my
ability to handle money. In each instance, it doesn't matter whether
I am good, or clever, or deserving—the only question is whether

I have the symbol of membership, whatever it may be. If I do, no matter how stupid or thoughtless or nasty I am, I get all the privileges of belonging.

Perhaps the most powerful example of this in history was the Passover. You probably know the story: Pharaoh has refused to set his slaves, the Israelites, free despite having his nation carpet bombed with frogs, gnats, boils, locusts, and the rest. Moses threatens that the firstborn of every Egyptian family will be killed unless he agrees to release his slaves. Pharaoh says no. So Yahweh sends the destroying angel through Egypt at night, killing every firstborn son, bringing catastrophic destruction and grief upon the nation. The Israelites, though, are protected from this plague in an extraordinary symbol of the grace of God:

> *Go and select lambs for yourselves according to your clans, and kill the Passover lamb. Take a bunch of hyssop and dip it in the blood that is in the basin, and touch the lintel and the two doorposts with the blood that is in the basin.... For Yahweh will pass through to strike the Egyptians, and when he sees the blood on the lintel and on the two doorposts, Yahweh will pass over the door and will not allow the destroyer to enter your houses to strike you. (Ex. 12:21–23)*

The only thing that separated the Israelites from death was the blood on their doorposts. They were not protected from destruction by good behavior, or ongoing obedience to God, or an elaborate deal by which they promised to follow him forever. Yet they were ransomed from death anyway. The blood on the doorpost made all the difference.

Just think for a moment about the scandal of this arrangement. In some cases, the Egyptians who were killed may have been better people than some of the Israelites who were saved. Looked at another way, the wicked Israelites received the same privileges as the godly ones, simply because they had blood on their doorposts. The blood on the doorpost wasn't another factor that God took into consideration when deciding who to rescue and who to destroy. It was the only one. Like the flashing blue light on the fire engine, the blood on the doorpost was the symbol of membership, and it made (quite literally) all the difference.

That is grace. It is how God works. So when we look at Jesus, our Passover Lamb who was sacrificed (1 Cor. 5:7), we see the same principle in operation. We see that our rescue from the slavery of sin is not based on our performance but on his sacrifice. We see that through faith in his blood, rather than through our efforts, we are not destroyed. We see that when the Father looks at our lives, he justifies us on the basis of Jesus' obedience and law-keeping and zeal for God, not on ours. The only factor, the *only* factor, that he takes into consideration is whether or not we have cried out for the blood of the Lamb, the blood of Jesus, to save us.

It makes all the difference.

THE CURTAIN

And Jesus cried out again with a loud voice and yielded up his spirit. And behold, the curtain of the temple was torn in two, from top to bottom. And the earth shook, and the rocks were split. —Matthew 27:50–51

Heaven and earth were separated by a curtain. It might not sound like much, but from Sinai to Calvary an embroidered sheet of twisted linen divided sinful people from their holy God. Every Israelite knew that Yahweh lived in their midst, but for fifteen centuries, all they could see was a curtain, up to sixty feet high and three inches thick.[1]

The curtain was a sign of separation. It kept the people apart from the awe-inspiring and dangerous Holy One on the other side, and reminded them that they were not up to the standard required to approach him. Occasionally in Israel's history, individuals forgot this and tried to approach Yahweh as if no curtain existed: out of defiance (Lev. 10:1–2), out of curiosity (1 Sam. 6:19–20), or even out of a misguided desire to help (2 Sam. 6:6–7). The instant death that met each one, while tragic for the individuals concerned, would have served as a warning to the rest of the people: God is profoundly holy, and you are not. So remember the curtain.

It first appeared around 1445 BC, when God gave Moses instructions on how to build the tabernacle. This huge tent had a courtyard about the size of an Olympic swimming pool, in which animal sacrifices were offered. At the back was a smaller structure, the Tent of Meeting, which only priests could enter, and this was marked off from the courtyard by a linen curtain, woven in blue, purple, and scarlet. Beyond this was a second curtain, sometimes called a "veil," which marked off the Holy of Holies. Only one man could go through this curtain, only once a year, and when he did, he attached golden bells to his robe so that he would not die (Ex. 28:35)! So actually, God was separated from the people by two curtains (although the New Testament often talks about them as if they are one), offering the people a powerful picture of how unapproachable Yahweh was. One curtain separating the people from the priests. Another curtain separating the priests from their God. Sixty feet high and three inches thick.

To illustrate this, think for a moment about the different security areas that you have in a bank. In the public spaces, open to everyone, there is very little real money. You know the money is in the bank somewhere, and you make transactions accordingly, but almost all of it is behind coded doors. Like the Israelites in the courtyard of the tabernacle, you cannot actually see the very thing you came for; you rely on others, who are authorized to act on your behalf, being able to access it for you. The bank staff, though, like the priests in Israel, are allowed through the coded doors into the secure areas. Most of the doors are at least six feet high and three inches thick.

But even the bank employees don't have access to the vault. Somewhere, deep inside the building, is a depository where millions of dollars are stored. It is maximum security, with a giant steel gate that can only be opened with a fingerprint and a retinal scan; only the chairman has access, and even he hardly ever goes inside. It is awkward for the chairman, inaccessible for the bank staff, and utterly impossible to get near for the likes of you and me. Even the first checkpoint is sixty feet high and three inches thick.

Now imagine you walk into your local bank, and all the coded doors are lying in pieces on the floor. As you peer through into the mysterious world on the other side, you can see an equally shattered steel gate, and behind it, all the money you could ever have imagined in nice neat piles. You wonder what you should do, until the chairman himself approaches you, tells you it is a new bank policy, and cheerfully invites you to go into the vault and help yourself to all the money you want.

Now change the picture: You are a temple attendant in AD 30. A beautifully embroidered curtain has isolated you from the presence of Yahweh for fifteen hundred years. Yet because of the death of Jesus of Nazareth, the barrier that prevented you approaching God has been destroyed forever, irrevocably torn from top to bottom. The Messiah's death was so definitive, his sacrifice so sufficient, that the very laws of physics could not hold together this mighty symbol of God's unapproachability, and it now lies ripped in half on the floor in front of you. Sixty feet high and three inches thick.

The curtain is torn. The animal sacrifices and bells and security codes and retinal scans are no longer needed; the vault of God's presence is open, and the Chairman is inviting us inside to enjoy it. So, as Hebrews 10:19–22 invites us, "since we have confidence to enter the holy places by the blood of Jesus, by the new and living way that he opened for us through the curtain … let us draw near with a true heart in full assurance of faith."

Endnote

1. Mishnah Shekalim, 8.5: "R. Simeon ben Gamaliel said, on account of R. Simeon, the son of the Sagan, the thickness of the veil is a handbreadth, and it is woven of seventy-two threads, and every thread has twenty-four threads in it. It is forty cubits long, and twenty broad."

THE DAY OF ATONEMENT

Then Aaron shall cast lots for the two goats: one lot for Yahweh and the other lot for the scapegoat. And Aaron shall bring the goat on which Yahweh's lot fell, and offer it as a sin offering. But the goat on which the lot fell to be the scapegoat shall be presented alive before Yahweh, to make atonement upon it, and to let it go as the scapegoat into the wilderness. —Leviticus 16:8–10 NKJV

What do the following phrases all have in common? A drop in the bucket; at his wits' end; bite the dust; by the skin of his teeth; give up the ghost; sour grapes; the powers that be; rise and shine. The answer is, they are all from the Bible but no longer have religious meanings, because they have entered everyday English. Maybe the best example of this, and certainly the most important in the biblical story, is the word we have just read in Leviticus 16: scapegoat.

It goes back three and a half thousand years to the Day of Atonement. This pivotal day in the Jewish calendar, still celebrated by Jews as *Yom Kippur*, was the day when the high priest entered the Most Holy Place to make atonement for the sins of the people. On no other day in the year was he allowed to do this; because of the holiness of God, if he did, he would die. On the Day of Atonement, though, he would take two goats, one for Yahweh and one for the scapegoat, and treat them completely differently, to symbolize the two things that happen when a holy God forgives a sinful people. One of them would be sacrificed and its blood smeared around the altar and the Holy Place, like a normal sin offering. The other is the scapegoat, and it would be sent out into the wilderness carrying the sins of the people, never to be seen again. It took the blame that rightly belonged to others, which is still what it means in secular English today.

It is important to understand that these two goats represented the two aspects of Yahweh's forgiveness: cleansing and separation. The first goat was all about cleansing from sin, and was primarily godward—it dealt with the uncleanness of sin and restored Israel to right relationship with Yahweh. Sin leads to death, which brings guilt, so our guilt is cleansed by the death of an innocent.

The scapegoat, on the other hand, was there to demonstrate separation from sin and was primarily humanward—it showed Israel that their sins had been taken away from them as far as the east is from the west, and that they would never see them again. Sin leads to separation, which brings shame; our shame is then removed by the exile of an innocent. For Israel's sake, and ours, both cleansing and separation are needed when God forgives, so that both guilt and shame are overcome. It's all very well having someone forgive you for theft, murder, or adultery, but if the result of your sin (a pile of stolen money, a corpse, a jilted husband) is sitting at the end of your bed when you wake up every day, it's far harder to accept it.

So the scapegoat is a very powerful picture. When the priest put his hands on the goat, laid Israel's sins upon it, and sent it into the desert, Israel knew that their transgressions had been not only forgiven but also forgotten; not just washed away from God's sight, but also taken away from ours. Picture it: As the goat was led out of the camp and into the wilderness, the people would be able to see all their jealousy and greed and lust and pride being walked out with it, and banished from their presence forever. One innocent animal effectively *became sin* for the people and left the camp to signify the complete removal of all shame.

Wonderfully, like so much else in Leviticus, both goats pointed forward to an even more dramatic picture of forgiveness:

> *For our sake he* made him to be sin *who knew no sin, so that in him we might become the righteousness of God. (2 Cor. 5:21)*

Now, I guess we're all happy with Jesus as the first goat, the sin offering that cleanses us before God. We sinned, he didn't, he got killed, we don't. It's true, it's glorious, and it's widely thought about, taught about, and sung about. But what we may not consider so often, but which is equally true, is that Jesus is our scapegoat: He took our sins upon himself and left the camp, separating us from our sins and removing the shame that separated us from God. Golgotha, where Jesus was crucified, was not a suburb of Jerusalem, but an execution venue outside the city walls. This may not seem significant to us, but to a Jewish person who understood Leviticus, it could not be more important:

> *For the bodies of those animals whose blood is brought into the holy places by the high priest as*

a sacrifice for sin are burned outside the camp.
So Jesus also suffered outside the gate in order
to sanctify the people through his own blood.
Therefore let us go to him outside the camp and
bear the reproach he endured. (Heb. 13:11–13)

Jesus was killed outside the city walls, outside the camp, to demonstrate that he was the way in which our sins were not just cleansed but also removed from us. As he walked out of the city that his power had founded, and of which he was the true king, carrying a cross and with his back ripped to shreds, he carried the shame of everything you and I have ever done. He carried it out of the camp, into the wilderness, onto the cross, never to be seen again. The ultimate scapegoat.

So the Day of Atonement was pretty amazing, really. It was a day of celebration and sins forgiven. It was the day on which God said the people should proclaim the Year of Jubilee (every fifty years), the year of property redistribution that showed the past was dealt with and everyone could start again. It demonstrated that those terrible consequences of sin, guilt and shame, were overcome. It showed that the effects of sin on both man and God had been atoned for, forgiven to the uttermost. And it pointed forward, in a spectacularly visual way, to another Day of Atonement and the astonishing reality that at the cross of Jesus, death would be killed and separation would be removed completely:

God presented him as a sacrifice of atonement,
through faith in his blood. (Rom. 3:25 NIV)

The Day of Atonement brought the Israelites complete forgiveness, because their sins were both killed and removed from them completely. In Jesus, we have ultimate, complete atonement because his sacrifice put our sins to death, once and for all (Heb. 10:10).

Psalm 103 was written when the old sacrifices were still being offered, but it gives an astonishing insight into the joy people have when their sins are taken away. You might like to use it as a prayer, remembering the total removal of all your wrongdoings by Jesus' death and resurrection.

> Bless Yahweh, O my soul, and all that is within me, bless his holy name! Bless Yahweh, O my soul, and forget not all his benefits, who forgives all your iniquity, who heals all your diseases, who redeems your life from the pit, who crowns you with steadfast love and mercy, who satisfies you with good so that your youth is renewed like the eagle's.

> Yahweh, you work righteousness and justice for all who are oppressed. You made known your ways to Moses, your acts to the people of Israel. You are merciful and gracious, slow to anger and abounding in steadfast love. You will not always chide, nor will you keep your anger forever. You do not deal with us according to our sins, nor repay us according to our iniquities.

> For as high as the heavens are above the earth, so great is your steadfast love toward those who fear you; as far as the east is from the west, so far do you

remove our transgressions from us. As a father shows compassion to his children, so you show compassion to those who fear you. For you know our frame; you remember that we are dust.

As for me, my days are like grass; I flourish like a flower of the field; for the wind passes over me, and I am gone, and my place knows it no more. But your steadfast love is from everlasting to everlasting on those who fear you, and your righteousness to children's children, to those who keep your covenant and remember to do your commandments. Yahweh, you have established your throne in the heavens, and your kingdom rules over all.

Bless Yahweh, O you his angels, you mighty ones who do his word, obeying the voice of his word! Bless Yahweh, all his hosts, his ministers, who do his will! Bless Yahweh, all his works, in all places of his dominion. Bless Yahweh, O my soul!

THE ARK OF THE COVENANT

They sent therefore and gathered together all the lords of the Philistines and said, "Send away the ark of the God of Israel, and let it return to its own place, that it may not kill us and our people." —1 Samuel 5:11

For a thousand years, God lived in a box. Theologians, don't freak out: I know that God fills heaven and earth, and that no box could contain him. But again and again in Scripture, a small box is described as housing the presence of Yahweh. It was made of acacia wood, was four feet long, two feet wide, and two feet high, and inside it were two stones with laws written on them, an urn with manna inside, and a staff that had sprouted flowers. It all sounds a bit peculiar to us, but that's where the power and presence of Yahweh could be found for around a millennium. It was called the ark of the covenant.

The journey of this box is one of my favorite GodStories, because it displays both the utter grace and the utter holiness of Yahweh. It shows his grace, because it indicates his desire to live among his people, even when they were stupid and sinful. Think about it: He could have chosen to remain up a fearsomely high and dangerous mountain, far removed from sinful humanity. If I'd been Yahweh, that's what I would have done. But instead, he decided to dwell in something portable, so that he could live among the people of God wherever they went. That's as unexpected as the CEO of Unilever having an office on the factory floor in Huddersfield, or the ambassador to India living in a Mumbai slum. The ark is a box of grace.

But it is also a box of holiness, and that's what most of this GodStory is about. When it is first built in the fifteenth century BC, Yahweh gives detailed instructions on how to build it, how to carry it, and how to approach it, because if man approaches the holiness of God without due care, he will die. Quickly, the Israelites discover that Yahweh's intense holiness means the box has tremendous power. When the priests carrying the ark reach the banks of the river Jordan, the river stops flowing, just like that. When they step out the other side, the river comes crashing back again and overflows its banks. When the ark is carried around Jericho, one of the ancient world's great fortified cities, the walls come crashing down. The ark of the covenant could save lives as well as destroy them, stop rivers as well as flood them, rescue Israel as well as trounce her enemies. It was quite a box.

This immense power, though, made it something of a talisman for Israel. They began to believe that the ark would save them independently of their disobedience, and started seeing the box as the source of power, rather than the God who dwelt within it. When you consider the holiness of Yahweh, it is no surprise that this "lucky charm" approach backfired spectacularly:

> *"Let us bring the ark of the covenant of Yahweh here from Shiloh, that it may come among us and save us from the power of our enemies." ... So*

the Philistines fought, and Israel was defeated,
and they fled, every man to his home.... And the
ark of God was captured. (1 Sam. 4:3, 10–11)

The ark of Yahweh was taken by the Philistines around 1100 BC. They knew that the box was where Israel's God lived, so they believed they would now have Yahweh fighting on their side. But a little knowledge is a dangerous thing, and they decided to put the ark in the temple of their god, Dagon. What the Philistines didn't know was that inside the box was the real God, the God of Abraham, Isaac, and Jacob, in all his unapproachable holiness. The result is predictable, and almost comic:

Behold, Dagon had fallen face downward on the
ground before the ark of Yahweh. So they took
Dagon and put him back in his place. But when
they rose early on the next morning, behold, Dagon
had fallen face downward on the ground before
the ark of Yahweh, and the head of Dagon and
both his hands were lying cut off on the threshold.
Only the trunk of Dagon was left to him. This is
why the priests of Dagon and all who enter the
house of Dagon do not tread on the threshold
of Dagon in Ashdod to this day. (1 Sam. 5:3–5)

I'm not surprised they didn't go back there—I wouldn't either. But it gets worse, because the entire town starts getting afflicted with tumors because of the ark. The Philistines respond with blind panic and send it on to the town next door, where the same thing happens, and then again in the town after that. Finally they get the message—that Yahweh is in the box, and he is not to be messed with—and send it back to Israel.

Even in Israel, the holiness of Yahweh and the box he lives in cause chaos. The first Israelites to see it make the mistake of peering inside, and seventy men in that village are killed. Terrified, they put it in the house of a man called Abinadab, where it remains for twenty years lest it kill anyone else. David, recently anointed king, then comes to bring the ark up to Jerusalem, and gets Abinadab's sons to drive the cart carrying it—but one of them, Uzzah, reaches out and touches the ark when the oxen stumble, and he is immediately killed as well. The ark may not be in a tabernacle at this point, but the God who lives within it is the same as he always has been. There is no room for a careless or flippant approach to the holiness of Yahweh—as Uzzah, son of Abinadab, would most surely have known.

After all that, and with much celebration, the ark arrives in Jerusalem around 1010, and it is eventually housed in Solomon's newly built temple around 950, with more sacrifices than can be counted. The box has lost none of its splendor over the last five centuries: When the box is placed in the temple, the glory cloud of Yahweh descends with such intensity that the priests are completely overwhelmed and left incapable of doing their jobs. And in the temple the ark remains, the focal point of Jewish worship and the centerpiece of Jewish hope.

That's not quite the end of the story though. When the Babylonians invade and drag Judah into exile, the ark is destroyed and looks like a total disaster. But the prophet Ezekiel, to his astonishment, sees the presence of Yahweh actually leaving the temple and coming to live

among the Jewish people, with God revealing his name as Yahweh-
is-there. Jeremiah goes further and prophesies that the ark will not
be rebuilt, or even pined for, in the age to come. So, though many
speculate about it, and Indiana Jones thought he found it, the ark of
the covenant is not on earth any longer. Instead, it is exactly where
you would expect it to be:

> *Then God's temple in heaven was opened, and the*
> *ark of his covenant was seen within his temple.*
> *There were flashes of lightning, rumblings, peals of*
> *thunder, an earthquake, and heavy hail. (Rev. 11:19)*

Presence and distance, grace and holiness. That's the ark. That's
our God.

THE TEMPLE

*When all the people of Israel saw the fire come
down and the glory of Yahweh on the temple, they
bowed down with their faces to the ground on
the pavement and worshiped and gave thanks to
Yahweh, saying, "For he is good, for his steadfast
love endures forever." —2 Chronicles 7:3*

In the beginning was the temple.[1]

That might sound like nonsense. Solomon's temple wasn't built until the eleventh century BC, and the world was created long before that. But if you look carefully through Scripture, you'll find that God's Word begins and ends with temples. You'll notice that temple imagery in the Bible is more about the presence of God than it is about any particular building, and that temple language tells a very clear GodStory about the presence of God filling the earth. After all, as Paul remarked in Acts 17:24, the God who made heaven and earth and everything else doesn't live in temples built by hands.

The garden of Eden was the original temple. It was the place where God lived and was a place of such holiness that sin could not remain within it. Like every temple, the garden had a priest, a man appointed to serve it and keep it, which are the exact same responsibilities Israel's priests would be given later in the story. As in

both the tabernacle and the temple in Jerusalem, the holy presence
of God in the garden was guarded by cherubim. Obviously, being a
garden, it was covered in fruit and had a tree in the middle; perhaps
less obviously, the tabernacle and the temple had designs that were
covered in fruit, and had a golden lampstand shaped like a tree in the
middle. Like the two main temple visions in Scripture, the garden
had a river flowing through the middle, and its entrance faced east.
I don't think all that can be coincidence. God set up the garden of
Eden as a sort of temple, with his presence right in the center.

So temples are there at the beginning of the GodStory. What
about at the end? Well, at the risk of spoiling it, read the vision of
the new heavens and the new earth in Revelation 21—22, and you'll
find that the whole of creation has become a temple. John sees the
new creation as a giant cubic structure—the same shape as the Most
Holy Place—where nothing unclean ever enters (like the temple).
The whole thing is written to remind people of the temple Ezekiel
saw, right down to the detail of the river:

> *And on the banks, on both sides of the river, there*
> *will grow all kinds of trees for food.... They will bear*
> *fresh fruit every month, because the water for*
> *them flows from the sanctuary. Their fruit will be*
> *for food, and their leaves for healing. (Ezek. 47:12)*

> *Also, on either side of the river, the tree of*
> *life with its twelve kinds of fruit, yielding its*
> *fruit each month. The leaves of the tree were*
> *for the healing of the nations. (Rev. 22:2)*

Pretty similar, aren't they? Yet there is a big difference, because in Revelation, the whole point is that the city has no temple. Instead, the whole of creation is filled with God's glory. In other words, *the entire new creation has become a temple*, a place where God lives in uninterrupted and untainted glory.

The Bible starts with the garden of Eden as a temple, with God in the middle, and ends with the whole earth as a temple, with God everywhere. The question is of course: So what? What did that mean for Israel, and what does it mean for us?

The temple was all about God's presence. When God instructed Moses to build a tabernacle, he told him to build it in three parts to illustrate this. There was the Most Holy Place (or the Holy of Holies), where God lived; the Holy Place (or the Tent of Meeting), where only priests could go; and the court, where normal Israelites could come. When the temple was built, it had the same structure, with three different layers of holiness, if you like. On one hand, Israel was able to benefit from having the presence of Yahweh in their midst, since the temple was where heaven met earth. That's why the scene we read at the beginning of this chapter is so dramatic; the presence of Yahweh filled the entire temple in glory and fire. On the other hand, the Jews were protected from Yahweh's holiness by being kept separate through this three-part system.

But this was never the ultimate plan. Remember, God's intention was that his presence could fill the whole earth, so the Jerusalem temple was only an interim measure. The bigger picture was that one day, the presence of God would break out of the Most Holy Place and start filling the entire cosmos, as had been the idea ever since Eden. With the cross of Jesus, this became possible. The ripping of the temple curtain not only brought the world into God's presence, but it also took God's presence into the world. Through Jesus, God's temple was suddenly expanding rapidly to fill the whole of creation.

That's where you and I come in:

> *Do you not know that you are God's temple and that God's Spirit dwells in you? If anyone destroys God's temple, God will destroy him. For God's temple is holy, and you are that temple. (1 Cor. 3:16–17)*

> *For we are the temple of the living God; as God said, "I will make my dwelling among them and walk among them, and I will be their God, and they shall be my people." (2 Cor. 6:16)*

> *You are ... built on the foundation of the apostles and prophets, Christ Jesus himself being the cornerstone, in whom the whole structure, being joined together, grows into a holy temple in the Lord. (Eph. 2:19–21)*

We are the way in which God's Spirit, the glory and the fire, fills the earth. The presence of God was concentrated in a garden, then a tent, then a temple, but now it is in the church of God. When Acts starts, the Most Holy Place is the size of an upper room; by the time Acts finishes, his presence has reached Rome. Today, it stretches from Antarctica to Alaska. But there is a day coming when it will fill the whole of creation, in one giant temple from Bethlehem to Betelgeuse:

> *The city has no need of sun or moon to shine on it, for the glory of God gives it light, and its lamp is the Lamb. By its light will the nations walk, and the kings of the earth will bring their glory into it. (Rev. 21:23–24)*

I can't wait.

Endnote

1. This chapter is based on the fascinating study of G. K. Beale, *The Temple and the Church's Mission* (Leicester: IVP, 2004).

ACT THREE
POETS AND PROPHETS

SUFFERING'S ANSWER

*Then Job arose and tore his robe and shaved his head
and fell on the ground and worshiped. And he said,
"Naked I came from my mother's womb, and naked
shall I return. Yahweh gave, and Yahweh has taken
away; blessed be the name of Yahweh." —Job 1:20-21*

If you've experienced suffering, you've got to love Job. I doubt anything ever written has been as brutally honest about the problem of pain in this life. All the difficult questions are raised, and all the easy answers are dismissed. All in all, it is one of the most profound, moving, and challenging GodStories there is.

In a nutshell, a good man experiences massive and inexplicable suffering. His possessions are destroyed by lightning and taken by raiders, his children are wiped out by a hurricane, and then he is covered in painful sores from head to toe. We then spend the rest of the poem exploring the various answers that can be given to the simple question: Why does suffering happen? Some of the answers are right, and some are wrong. So in this narrative, we're going to learn as much as we can from Job's experience, and then reflect on what it means for a world rife with child abuse and ethnic cleansing and sex slavery and tsunamis. We're going to try and find suffering's answer.

First, let's look at some of the wrong answers. Lots of easy explanations that people give (and that we may have given ourselves!) are torpedoed by the book of Job, of which we can only mention four.

1. Suffering isn't real. This is the Buddhist response to the problem of evil: Suffering is an illusion, so we don't need to explain it. Job does not go near such a silly answer, and the writer pulls no punches in saying both how real and how unpleasant human suffering can often be. Making light of bereavement or cancer doesn't make them go away.

2. God doesn't cause suffering; Satan does. Although this is often said, and it seems to help, it comes at a massive cost, because it implies that God is not really in control—he's officially in power, like King Richard in *Robin Hood*, but unable to stop the Sheriff of Nottingham running riot. A friend of mine had a series of problems buying a house recently and told me that whenever things went right, people said "Praise God!" but when they went wrong, they told him it was opposition from the Devil. This is not always true. And it certainly wasn't for Job: "Yahweh gave, and Yahweh has taken away; blessed be the name of Yahweh."

3. God is not good. This is the conclusion that some atheists have come to in recent years, and it is also the response of Job's wife, who urges Job to curse God and die. Job will not have any of it: "Shall we receive good from God, and shall we not receive evil?" (2:10). God's goodness is not on the table. There must be another reason.

4. We get what we deserve; so if you're suffering, it's your fault. This, to oversimplify, is where Job's three friends are coming from; they start down this line of reasoning early on and get more and more strident about it as the poem continues. But this, apart from

being a very unpleasant thing to say to someone in pain, is also wrong, because good people like Job sometimes suffer, and wicked people sometimes prosper (21:7). People who preach a gospel of health, wealth, and prosperity for all God's children have simply not reckoned with Job, let alone Jesus.

Although the book of Job raises and dismisses a number of bad responses to suffering, it also gives several good ones, which we would do well to learn from.

1. Silence. This is how Job's friends begin, and it is absolutely appropriate. When someone has lost his or her family, possessions, and health, a cheerful "It'll be okay" is useless. Sitting with them, sharing their grief, and waiting in silence is far better.

2. God is still in charge, and God is still good, even though his idea of goodness might not always be the same as mine. Despite Job's terrible pain and confusion, both he and his friends hold fast to these truths. In contrast, if I am honest, I can sometimes try to make God smaller to account for things I don't understand. We mustn't purchase our answers at the expense of either God's goodness or his sovereignty.

3. Resurrection is coming. This is an extraordinary piece of revelation that hits Job about halfway through the book, and while it doesn't make suffering go away, it certainly helps put it in perspective. When Job starts out, he believes that death is the end, the grave is a one-way street, and therefore suffering in this life will have the last word. When resurrection is factored in, though, there is hope of a better future: "I know that my Redeemer lives, and at the last he will stand upon the earth. And after my skin has been thus destroyed, yet in my flesh I shall see God" (19:25–26).

4. Yahweh is far, far greater than we are, and has purposes in the world we know nothing about. This, ultimately, is the answer given by Yahweh himself: There are millions of things taking place every second that you and I know nothing about, from thunderbolts being sent in the Cook Islands to mountain goats giving birth in Tibet; all of them are orchestrated by almighty God. So if ecological disasters and economic depressions take place at times and we don't understand why, it is not surprising. We found electricity only a few years back, and we still can't figure out how to make even one living cell. As Job admits, "I have uttered what I did not understand, things too wonderful for me, which I did not know" (42:3).

Now, all of this is useful. It may help us cope with suffering ourselves, comfort others, and praise God through dark times. But in themselves, they are mere signposts in the fog, hints of an answer that has not yet come. And the reason for this is that the ultimate answer to suffering is not an argument or an idea, but a person. Suffering's answer is Jesus.

Job hints at this. In 9:32–33, he expresses anguish that God is not a man, as we are, so there is no arbiter between us and the Almighty. Then, in 23:3–7, he cries out for God's judgment throne to be within reach, so that he could have his case tried in court. Job believes his suffering would be answered if God could simply become man, relate to human suffering, and make his judgment throne available to man. Perhaps the writer to the Hebrews had this in mind when he said this of Jesus:

> For we do not have a high priest who is unable
> to sympathize with our weaknesses, but one who

in every respect has been tempted as we are, yet
without sin. Let us then with confidence draw near
to the throne of grace, that we may receive mercy
and find grace to help in time of need. (Heb. 4:15–16)

Imagine all humanity had a committee meeting to establish what God would have to go through to truly understand human suffering. The poor would say he should be homeless, frequently hungry, and constantly moving from place to place. Bereaved people would say he should lose a parent and perhaps a close friend as well. Holocaust victims might insist he be Jewish; those who lived in occupied territories, that he should live his entire life in subjection to a brutal empire. Outcasts would insist he face a major social stigma: accusations of illegitimacy or drunkenness or demon-possession. The abused might demand he face physical violence, ritual humiliation, abandonment, and betrayal by those closest to him, and yet with the perpetrators never punished. I don't know what you would throw in—never having children, being murdered in his prime, or perhaps facing extended torture and slow death. Maybe those who had felt the silence of heaven, like Job, would add that to the list, to form the most profound and wide-ranging suffering imaginable. Then and only then, humanity might say, could God be regarded as being able to understand our suffering. Only if God had lived through the worst this life had to offer and been perfect throughout could we say he had provided Suffering's Answer.

Sound like anyone we know?

COFFEE BREAK:

WAIT AND WORSHIP

. . . .

If you are suffering, there are no easy answers. But one of our great sources of comfort is the massive lineup of those disciples who, through the centuries, have struggled with terrible suffering and yet continued to praise their God. The great Puritan John Owen lost ten out of his eleven children in infancy but wrote some of the most outstanding material on the person of Christ ever written. David Brainerd, missionary to the Native Americans of New England, died of tuberculosis at the young age of twenty-nine, but his diary shows a man of extraordinary joy in God.

One of the most famous songs of worship through suffering was written by Horatio Spafford in 1873. His only son died in 1871, and then the great Chicago fire brought him to financial ruin. Two years later, his four daughters all died in a shipping collision in the Atlantic, prompting him to write the following words. People who know their God can respond to trials in the most amazing ways!

> When peace, like a river, attendeth my way,
> When sorrows like sea billows roll;
> Whatever my lot, Thou hast taught me to say,
> It is well, it is well, with my soul.
>
> Though Satan should buffet, though trials
>   should come,
> Let this blest assurance control,
> That Christ has regarded my helpless estate,
> And hath shed His own blood for my soul.
>
> My sin, oh, the bliss of this glorious thought!
> My sin, not in part but the whole,

Is nailed to the cross, and I bear it no more,
Praise the Lord, praise the Lord, O my soul!

And Lord, haste the day when my faith shall be
    sight,
The clouds be rolled back as a scroll;
The trumpet shall sound, and the Lord shall
    descend,
Even so, it is well with my soul.

THE SHADOW OF THE CROSS

*My God, my God, why have you
forsaken me? —Psalm 22:1*

If Psalm 22 doesn't get your heart racing, you need to check your pulse. It gives insight into the suffering of Jesus like almost nothing else, it links together David and Christ with startling originality, and it proves beyond any doubt that God knows the future. In thirty-one verses, we are given detail after detail about the cross that no one but God could possibly have known, and yet the psalm still ends on a note of triumph rather than tragedy. The Messiah will suffer, it tells us, but he will be vindicated.

The psalm begins with a very famous line: "My God, my God, why have you forsaken me?" Originally written by David, probably while on the run from Saul, this deep cry of anguish is quoted in Aramaic by Jesus on the cross, which tells us two things. It tells us that David was prefiguring what would happen to Jesus, and it tells us Jesus was fulfilling what had happened to David. These are subtly different. David is saying, quite unconsciously, that the Messiah, the true King and the true servant of Yahweh, will suffer. That is very interesting, and it is not what most Jews would have expected. But Jesus is saying, quite consciously, that he is that Messiah, the King in the line of David, and that his suffering is exactly what you should expect if you had read your Old Testament properly. (It also suggests his abandonment by the Father, but that is not the main point.) To the crowds jeering at him on the cross, the fact that he had been strung up and humiliated was proof that he was not Israel's Savior. With his quotation of Psalm 22:1, however, Jesus shows it was proof that he was.

On its own, there might not be anything too remarkable about that. Presumably anyone could quote David as they were dying and claim that they were the Messiah. But as the psalm progresses, we notice links between David and Christ that could not possibly have happened except by the power and knowledge of God, since they involved numerous other people's choices. Taken together, they show that Jesus was right: He was the son of David, he was Israel's Messiah, he was the King of the Jews (as, ironically, the piece of wood above his head said he was), and he would be vindicated by God after his suffering.

The first link is the reaction of Jesus' onlookers. David put it this way: "All who see me mock me; they make mouths at me; they wag their heads; 'He trusts in Yahweh; let him deliver him; let him rescue him, for he delights in him!'" Jump forward a thousand years, and you find this prophecy fulfilled exactly:

> And those who passed by derided him, wagging their heads.... So also the chief priests, with the scribes and elders, mocked him, saying, "He saved others; he cannot save himself. He is the King of Israel.... He trusts in God; let God deliver him now, if he desires him." (Matt. 27:39–43)

The second link is the extent of Jesus' suffering. The idea of a righteous king of Israel going through intense pain and anguish would have been very surprising to people, but David gives no room for doubt: "I am poured out like water, and all my bones are out of joint … my tongue sticks to my jaws; you lay me in the dust of death." David was prophesying a type of persecution that would lead to the dislocation of bones, intense thirst, and ultimately death. He could not have known that the Christ would experience all three, and he would not have known what to make of it if he did, since a dead Messiah was as unthinkable as a square circle. Furthermore, if you look carefully, when Jesus said "I thirst" and was given wine mixed with vinegar, it was not so much a statement of fact as a statement of fulfillment, both of this prophecy and of another of David's suffering psalms:

> They gave me poison for food, and for my thirst
> they gave me sour wine to drink. (Ps. 69:21)

Jesus was the King in the line of David, so he experienced all the sufferings David talked about. Even to death.

The third link is the most remarkable of all and concerns the details of Jesus' suffering. David writes that evildoers are gathered round him and "have pierced [his] hands and feet." This gives me the shivers, because it was written not just a thousand years before Jesus was crucified—his hands and feet pierced with six-inch metal spikes—but five hundred years before crucifixion was even invented. You wonder whether David had any idea what he was saying, since no form of execution known to man at that time would have involved pierced hands and feet. Two verses later, David says that his tormentors "divide my garments among them, and for my clothing they cast lots." This is incredible: It predicts a method of execution where the victim is naked, the clothes Jesus would be wearing on the night of his betrayal, and (once again) the decisions made and games played by Roman soldiers who had not yet been born and had never read a single psalm. Yet there these prophecies are in Psalm 22, an array of jarring and wonderful predictions that testify to the sovereignty and foreknowledge of the God who had already planned the cross.

All of these prophecies, though, are not the main point of the psalm. For that, we need to look at the ending, where the vindication of both Israel's King and Israel's God are announced, and the worship of the nations is promised:

> All the ends of the earth shall remember and turn to Yahweh, and all the families of the nations shall worship before you. For kingship belongs to Yahweh, and he rules over the nations.... They shall come and proclaim his righteousness to a people yet unborn, that he has done it. (Ps. 22:27–28, 31)

Astounding. David prophesies that, through the suffering of the King, the ends of the earth will turn to Yahweh, and the families of the nations will worship him, in fulfillment of the promise to Abraham and in prediction of the Great Commission. What started off as a dirge about being forgotten has turned into a jig about being remembered, and the psalm fittingly ends with the promise that people not yet born will celebrate that "he has done it."

That's you. You fulfill Psalm 22 every time you praise God on your own, every time you break bread with other believers, every time you talk about Jesus to those who don't yet know him. Every time you proclaim that "he has done it." That it is finished.

SINS FORGIVEN

*Purge me with hyssop, and I shall be clean; wash
me, and I shall be whiter than snow. Let me hear
joy and gladness; let the bones that you have
broken rejoice. Hide your face from my sins,
and blot out all my iniquities. —Psalm 51:7-9*

Whiter than snow. Only two people could use a phrase like that, and
only one of them could mean it. The first is a marketing executive for
Procter and Gamble, and the second is someone who has experienced
the swamping, sweeping forgiveness of Yahweh. I have been both, so
I know the first is a rather silly exaggeration to sell washing powder.
The second, on the other hand, is one of the most profound realities
in the universe.

I'm sure there are a wide variety of people reading this book, with
a whole range of sins in our pasts, but I doubt many have committed
both adultery and murder in the last couple of weeks. But that is where
David, who wrote the verses we have just read, is coming from. By
my count, based on what we read in 2 Samuel 11—12, David had
just broken eight of the ten commandments, yet here he is, praying
to Yahweh for restoration and using phrases like "clean," "whiter
than snow," "joy and gladness," and "rejoice." You might think he is
deluded, or cheeky, or at least a bit optimistic, but he isn't. In fact, he
understands Yahweh's forgiveness better than we do.

We probably struggle believing that. At a commonsense level, it just doesn't seem right, because we forgive people proportionately to the crime: If someone steps on your foot, no problem, but to forgive a rapist or a war criminal would take longer. Yahweh doesn't work like that, though. Every sin is an act of idolatry, and every sin requires God to be overwhelmingly gracious if there is to be forgiveness. Therefore David has every reason to think that God will forgive him—not because his sin is acceptable, but because his God is merciful. That's how grace works. It is based on God's character, not on ours. And it involves the *total* eradication of *every* sin we repent of.

The word-pictures David uses are his attempts to explain quite how dramatic this is. Take the phrase "whiter than snow," for example. I am writing this book in Atlantic Canada in February, and the province is basically one giant snowdrift. It was hardly snowing when I got home last night, though, so as I drove up my road, the car left a pair of dirty brown tracks behind me, like scars on the otherwise pure white landscape. Our sins are like that: dirty smears that taint the world we live in and are painfully obvious to others. When I got up this morning, however, those tracks were rendered completely invisible by a perfect blanket of fresh snow that had fallen overnight. It looked like the road had been ironed; not only had my tracks been covered, but you would never be able to find them even if you wanted to. And if I drive out today and add new tire marks, they'll be as white as snow all over again tomorrow. And the day after that. And the day after that. The snow, like God's grace, is new every morning, so no amount of black marks—not even the massive ones that are made by the snowplow vehicles, or the hideous messes we make of our relationships and finances—will withstand the whiteness of God's forgiveness.

The next image David uses for forgiveness is that of joy. Even those of us who can accept the snow picture might find this one troubling—how can such disgusting sin lead to so much joy that "broken bones rejoice"? But the greater the sin we commit, the greater the joy at finding forgiveness and the greater the love we feel toward the forgiver. Jesus makes this point in one of his most punchy parables:

> A certain moneylender had two debtors. One owed five hundred denarii, and the other fifty. When they could not pay, he cancelled the debt of both. Now which of them will love him more? (Luke 7:41–42)

The more you have been forgiven, the happier you are about it. So for a sinner to ask for forgiveness and not expect joy is like a parched man asking for a drink and not expecting refreshment. We're supposed to enjoy being forgiven.

We probably have a fair idea of what "hide your face from my sins" might mean, so let's jump to the final description of forgiven sins in these verses: "blot out all my iniquities." Remarkably, David calls on Yahweh not just to cover his sins, but to erase them completely (the same word is used of the creatures obliterated in the flood, for instance). More remarkably, this is exactly what God does, remembering our sins no more, separating them from us like east from west, and so on. The very worst things we have done are destroyed, blotted out, never to reappear.

Yet even David did not understand quite how completely our sins are forgiven. You see, our sins are not just canceled, leaving a blank instead of a debit. They are replaced, overwritten, leaving a credit instead of a debit. When God forgives you of your sins, he doesn't take you from negative one million to zero. He takes you from negative one million to a credit of one hundred million, crediting you with righteousness and decimating your sins forever. I don't know whether you've ever deleted a file on your computer, only to find that it's still hovering around in your Recycle Bin, or backed up on your server, a year later. That is what sin can be like to us—we can forget it for a while, but it often bounces back into our minds and makes us feel guilty again. IT technicians tell me, however, that the way to get rid of files forever is to write over them with something else, replacing their content with new stuff. Once you've overwritten a file, the old version is completely removed from the hard drive. And that, wonder of wonders, is what sin is like to God. He overwrites our sins with his righteousness and removes it completely from his memory.

All in all, forgiveness is pretty extraordinary. It deletes sins and delights sinners, leaving you, me, and David with clear records and clean hearts. Whether you're a murderer, a rapist, a pedophile, or an idolater, forgiveness of sins is available if you repent. No wonder David sang so much.

REALITY CHECK

*We have all become like one who is
unclean, and all our righteous deeds are
like a polluted garment. —Isaiah 64:6*

I have good news for you: You're far worse than you think.

To most people, that would probably sound like bad news. Most people want to think that they are fairly good, and it is not usually welcome to tell them otherwise. But in some situations, discovering that you are far worse than you think can be excellent news. If you were refusing to see a doctor because you didn't think your lump was anything to worry about, then discovering it was cancerous would actually be good news, because it would help you remove the problem. So it depends on the circumstances. Thinking you're good at something might simply be confidence, but it might also be foolishness.

When it comes to our standing before God, we need an accurate assessment of ourselves. Just as we wouldn't mess around with cancer, so we should not with the living God. You see, there will come a day when every one of us will stand before King Jesus and be answerable for what we have done (2 Cor. 5:10); and on that day, there will be nowhere to hide and no way to argue our way out of our mistakes. So finding out now that we are far worse than we thought is actually a good thing. It means we will not come unstuck when we stand before the judge of heaven and earth.

Evangelist Phil Moore refers to this reality check as the Simon Cowell moment. In the UK television show *X Factor* and its American counterpart, *American Idol*, showbiz hopefuls from all around the country audition for the chance to get on television and sing, with the winner securing a record deal at the end of the series. Unfortunately, many of the contestants who appear on the show have an inflated view of their musical ability. Some of them are simply appalling and yet have no idea how bad they sound, perhaps as a result of an enthusiastic family, a shower with generous acoustics, and the odd fact that none of us truly hear ourselves as we sound to others. Blissfully ignorant, these poor contestants then sing on television sounding like strangled sheep, all the while believing they are Beyoncé reborn.

Then they face Simon Cowell. After their performance, the feisty record producer gives them a blunt and often withering review, in which the insults fly and the showbiz hopeful comes crashing back to earth. While the whole thing is dramatized for entertainment, the main reason the contestants tend to look so crushed at this point is that they encounter a sudden reality check. In their world, compared to their friends and their family, they had sounded fantastic—but now, with the world watching and in front of the only man who really matters, they are shown to be rather less talented than they thought.

Jesus, of course, is no Simon Cowell. The purpose of the exercise is justice, not humiliation; the driving force behind the decision is expensive grace, not cheap laughs. Yet from our point of view, as ordinary folks with an unjustifiably high opinion of our righteousness, the experience will be much the same. Compared with our family and our friends in our little world—in which we judge others by their actions and ourselves by our intentions—we may seem very righteous indeed. But on that day, with heaven watching and in front of the only One who really matters, we will be shown to be rather less righteous than we thought.

Isaiah's wonderful phrase for this is "all our righteous deeds are like a polluted garment." To be honest, the translation here slightly softens the original, which has the same words you would use for menstrual rags: soiled, spoiled, ruined, filthy scraps of material, lacking any outward beauty at all, ceremonially unclean, and worthy of being thrown away or burned. Yet this is the analogy Isaiah uses for the very best efforts of sinful people. Compared to one another, our "righteous deeds" might gain us brownie points, but compared to God, they are like a used sanitary towel. A sheep seems very white when compared to the rest of the farmyard, but put it in a snowy field and it looks decidedly yellow.

How, then, can this be good news? If our best efforts are useless, then what is the point of anything? Well, two things need to be said here. The first is that, in Isaiah 64, Isaiah is talking about the righteous deeds of people without God: people who have been in sin for ages (v. 5) and who do not call on his name (v. 7). So we need not conclude that there is no way, ever, for people to please God; it is just that pleasing God is impossible without trusting in him for help (Heb. 11:6). If we know that the Simon Cowell moment is coming, we are far more likely to call out to God for rescue.

The second thing, which is far more wonderful, is that this

sort of predicament, based on the massive limitations of our own righteousness, means we require a righteousness that is not our own. Think about it: If our righteous deeds are woefully inadequate (as Isaiah says here), yet many people are still destined to be counted righteous (as he said in 53:11), then *that righteousness must come from somewhere.* If you said to your child that they were going to get 13,000 feet up Mont Blanc, but that they had no chance of making it climbing, then they would tremble with excitement, because it would suggest they were riding a train, or perhaps a cable car. In the same way, the promise of God that righteousness is available, coupled with the fact that my good deeds don't get me anywhere, indicates that righteousness will come to me from beyond myself, and that my standing before God will be based on the actions of someone else. Someone better.

But that is another GodStory.

THE ARM OF YAHWEH

Who has believed what he has heard
from us? And to whom has the arm of
Yahweh been revealed? —Isaiah 53:1

Four years ago, my friend Chris shot me in the face. We were in a friend's flat, in the kitchen, and he pointed a BB gun at me and pulled the trigger. He claims that he didn't think there was a pellet in it; whether or not that's true, there certainly was. A small, hard plastic ball hit me in the cheek at point-blank range, and it was extremely painful. Unknown to us, there was a man in the car park below our window who had seen the whole thing—Chris pointing a gun at me and firing, then me reeling in pain and shouting, "You shot me in the face!"—and had called the police. The police took the threat seriously and arrived at the flat at three a.m., bursting into my friend's bedroom through the fire exit in full riot gear. Half asleep and very confused, my friend had no idea why they kept asking him where the gun was. When he finally realized they must have mistaken his BB gun for a real one, he picked it up to show them and was greeted with three rifles pointed at him to cries of "Drop the gun! Drop the gun!" The police finally accepted that it was a toy, but not before they had scared the living daylights out of everybody. They had come prepared for violent confrontation and were quite disoriented when it turned out to be something else.

Isaiah's confusion and astonishment in the verse above may have been similar to the officers'. You probably noticed that Isaiah's words express complete amazement at what he can see: "Who has believed it? To whom has it been revealed?" These are the questions of someone who has received revelation from God but cannot quite bring himself to believe it yet. They are the questions of someone who knows that "the arm of Yahweh" means destruction and warfare are in the cards, and who has just heard from God that his arm will include his own suffering and his sacrificial death. Not surprisingly, Isaiah can't quite square the circle.

You see, "the arm of Yahweh" always meant blood and judgment. In Exodus 6:6, God promised deliverance by his outstretched arm, and within weeks there came a series of plagues that make *Outbreak* look like a tea party. When the phrase next appears, the scene is more reminiscent of *Braveheart*, as an entire army gets wiped out in front of Israelites singing, "Terror and dread fall upon them; because of the greatness of your arm, they are still as a stone" (Ex. 15:16). So when Isaiah 52:10 promises, "Yahweh has bared his holy arm before the eyes of all the nations," you could be forgiven for thinking that the war to end all wars was coming. But that is not what happens.

Instead, Isaiah describes the arm of Yahweh as a *servant*. As his lens comes into focus in Isaiah 52:13—53:12, we see a servant so physically disfigured that you cannot tell what his face looks like: a man of sorrows, despised by other people, the sort of person that you hide your face from and pretend you haven't seen, like the toothless addict who asks you for money outside the bank. Who has believed it? Or to whom has the arm of Yahweh been revealed?

Isaiah, looking on at this strange scene of a battered servant with whom no one made eye contact, couldn't help spluttering in disbelief. Remember the riot police at my friend's flat? Based on their history and experience—when you hear about someone being shot, it usually means a violent showdown is approaching—they were shocked to find a person in pajamas carrying a plastic pistol. In the same way, Isaiah, based on his history and experience—when you hear about the arm of Yahweh, it usually means a violent showdown is approaching—was shocked to find a suffering servant wielding a cross. In that cross, however, was a victory more profound and everlasting than any other, one that astonished people then and bamboozles them now. For in that cross, once and for all, God bared his holy arm in the sight of all the nations and ground wickedness into the dust.

This is one of Scripture's most surprising twists. The arm of Yahweh was still working rescue for God's people, but in a totally new way. Destruction, blood, and judgment were still there, but the destruction was that of transgressions, the blood that of a sacrifice, and the judgment poured out on the only person who didn't deserve it. God's arm was brandished and ready for battle, but the fight was not with sinful people but with sin itself. The battleground of the whole scene was Jesus: the fist and the punching bag, the Servant King, the arm of Yahweh in human form. But in the end, the result was the same: victory for God and the spoils of battle to his Son (53:12).

Arm of Yahweh, one; sin and death, nil.

A NEW SPIRIT

I will sprinkle clean water on you, and you shall be clean from all your uncleannesses, and from all your idols I will cleanse you. And I will give you a new heart, and a new spirit I will put within you. And I will remove the heart of stone from your flesh and give you a heart of flesh. And I will put my Spirit within you, and cause you to walk in my statutes and be careful to obey my rules. —Ezekiel 36:25–27

I'll be honest with you: I find reading the prophets very hard work sometimes. I've been going through them in my devotional times while writing this book, and again and again I have been confronted with long passages promising nothing but judgment. They can be quite depressing and a bit overwhelming. How are we supposed to respond to endless chapters explaining how Israel, Judah, and pretty much everyone else are going to be destroyed because of disobedience? What am I meant to learn from the ongoing cycle of sin and punishment? The sinfulness of man, obviously; the holiness of God, certainly. But although I know those themes are there, I cannot help but respond to the prophecies of judgment like an emperor penguin responds to the Antarctic winter—with persistent endurance, with gritted teeth, waiting for the light to break.

Yet the light always breaks. That's the beauty of the prophets.

They are so sure of Yahweh's unceasing and steadfast love that they know things won't always be like this. Even when Israel is fighting Judah, kings are worshipping false gods, and there are idols and phallic symbols "on every high hill and under every green tree," Yahweh is still true. He still keeps his covenant with Abraham. So the prophets know that, ultimately, God is going to change things. It will have to be his initiative, because the people keep flunking it. It will have to involve some fairly dramatic changes to the way humanity works, because even God's chosen people don't seem to be able to obey him, let alone everyone else. But the alternative—humanity being left to their own devices, abandoned by God and rotting in sin—is unthinkable. God is faithful.

Welcome to Ezekiel's world. This priest-turned-prophet had the tough task of speaking to the Jews in exile, after centuries of decline and disobedience had led to them being invaded, besieged, taken captive, and marched across the Middle East to Babylon, in what is now Iraq. The ungodliness of the people is shocking: Israel and Judah have prostituted themselves to false gods, there are idols in the temple, people are worshipping the sun, and there are abominations everywhere. So Ezekiel's book is filled with judgment on Judah for their sins, some of which is so graphic it found its way into *Pulp Fiction* (fire, vengeance, slaughter, famine, disease, and the rest), and to top it all off, the temple is destroyed by the Babylonians in 587 BC. All in all, it is a fairly dark hour for the people of God.

But the darkest hour is just before the dawn. Just as we are thinking that human beings will never walk in God's ways on their own, Ezekiel reveals Yahweh's astonishing answer: that human beings will indeed never walk in God's ways on their own, so they will be given completely new hearts and spirits. I will sprinkle clean water on you, Yahweh says. I will take out your old heart and give you a new one. No longer will you be hard like stone, but soft like flesh; in fact, I am going to put my Spirit inside you, and he will cause you to follow my ways like you've never done before. I am going to take the initiative, and it will change you forever.

In spite of the way we often talk, you see, you and I are incapable of pleasing God without the Holy Spirit living in us. It's not that it's difficult; it's impossible. Telling me to walk in God's ways with my natural heart of stone is like telling an apple tree to produce oranges. The apple tree can strain and go to an accountability group and screw its eyes up tightly, but it is never going to produce oranges unless it is given completely new DNA. We're like that. Our hearts of stone, try as we might, are not going to bring about obedience to God; instead we need completely new DNA—the Spirit of God within us, in every cell, so that we may live to please him. Without the Spirit, the Christian life would be impossible, a futile life of straining and accountability groups and screwing our eyes up tightly. With the Spirit, though, we produce godliness as naturally as an orange tree makes oranges.

Lots of people are baffled by this, because it sounds like there's nothing we can do by our own effort; it's all a question of being given something by God. It is. That's exactly what Ezekiel 36 is about; the history of Israel is a diary of life without the Spirit, and it doesn't work. Our only hope of producing God-honoring behavior is, Ezekiel says, to be sprinkled with clean water, given a soft heart of flesh, and given the Spirit to live within us. This is where Jesus was coming from when he announced to an equally baffled Pharisee:

Truly, truly, I say to you, unless one is born of water
and the Spirit, he cannot enter the kingdom of God.
That which is born of the flesh is flesh, and that
which is born of the Spirit is spirit. (John 3:5-6)

That's not to say that obedience is automatic. There are disobedient people in the New Testament church, just like there are some obedient people in the Old Testament church. (In that sense, we are different from the orange tree, because we have the choice to ignore our new DNA.) But if obedience isn't automatic with the Holy Spirit, it isn't difficult, either. In fact, it comes naturally as we walk with him. I cannot count the number of people I know who have become Christians and then, without ever being told what to do, have stopped doing drugs and swearing and getting drunk and sleeping around—not by straining or by being threatened, but by walking in the Spirit. That's because God gives us new DNA, a new heart and a new spirit, not a new rule book or a new method. It's because he makes us want different things, not just strive for them; he gives us new desires, not just new disciplines.

Ezekiel, who lived six centuries before the Holy Spirit came to live in people like this, would have loved to be where you are today. He would have relished the chance to be given a new spirit, like you have, and he would have daydreamed of what might happen if the whole of Israel was given one. No more idolatry, no more abominations, no more prophecies of judgment, just a glorious GodStory of new creation, delighted obedience, and a new spirit. The light always breaks.

It's great to understand the theology of "a new spirit," but what about the practice? How does it actually work in my daily life? Well, this is something addressed by Paul in two particular places. Read through them slowly, compare the two passages, and get a vision for what life in the Spirit looks like in reality.

Romans 8:5–14

> *For those who live according to the flesh set their minds on the things of the flesh, but those who live according to the Spirit set their minds on the things of the Spirit. For to set the mind on the flesh is death, but to set the mind on the Spirit is life and peace. For the mind that is set on the flesh is hostile to God, for it does not submit to God's law; indeed, it cannot. Those who are in the flesh cannot please God.*

> *You, however, are not in the flesh but in the Spirit, if in fact the Spirit of God dwells in you. Anyone who does not have the Spirit of Christ does not belong to him. But if Christ is in you, although the body is dead because of sin, the Spirit is life because of righteousness. If the Spirit of him who raised Jesus from the dead dwells in you, he who raised Christ Jesus from the dead will also give life to your mortal bodies through his Spirit who dwells in you.*

> *So then, brothers, we are debtors, not to the flesh, to*

*live according to the flesh. For if you live according
to the flesh you will die, but if by the Spirit you put
to death the deeds of the body, you will live. For all
who are led by the Spirit of God are sons of God.*

Galatians 5:16–25

*But I say, walk by the Spirit, and you will not gratify
the desires of the flesh. For the desires of the flesh
are against the Spirit, and the desires of the Spirit are
against the flesh, for these are opposed to each other,
to keep you from doing the things you want to do.*

*But if you are led by the Spirit, you are not
under the law. Now the works of the flesh are
evident: sexual immorality, impurity, sensuality,
idolatry, sorcery, enmity, strife, jealousy, fits
of anger, rivalries, dissensions, divisions, envy,
drunkenness, orgies, and things like these. I warn
you, as I warned you before, that those who do
such things will not inherit the kingdom of God.*

*But the fruit of the Spirit is love, joy, peace, patience,
kindness, goodness, faithfulness, gentleness, self-
control; against such things there is no law. And
those who belong to Christ Jesus have crucified
the flesh with its passions and desires. If we live
by the Spirit, let us also walk by the Spirit.*

A NEW COVENANT

"The time is coming," declares Yahweh, "when I will make a new covenant with the house of Israel and with the house of Judah ... I will put my law in their minds and write it on their hearts. I will be their God, and they will be my people. No longer will a man teach his neighbor, or a man his brother, saying, 'Know Yahweh,' because they will all know me, from the least of them to the greatest," declares Yahweh. "For I will forgive their wickedness and will remember their sins no more." —Jeremiah 31:31–34 (NIV)

By my reckoning, Jeremiah had a pretty awful job. He had to prophesy at length about the destruction of Jerusalem while he was still living there, knowing that the darkest moment in Israel's history was coming right around the corner like an unseen juggernaut, and weeping that the people of Israel were going to crash right into it because they weren't going to listen to a word he said. In the circumstances, what's surprising is not how distressed he was, but how hopeful.

I say that because the verses we just read are in many ways the most profound and sweeping expression of hope in the entire Old Testament. They speak of something that, in the context, was spectacularly improbable: a new covenant to replace the law of Moses. It's hard to grasp how unlikely this was, because not many things in our culture are as old as the law of Moses was; the first covenant was older then than the English language is now. Not only that, but God had also established the covenant with Moses and confirmed it with a whole array of terrifying signs and wonders. It would be like predicting that the Faeroe Islands were going to win the World Cup or that the giant panda was going to overtake the beetle as the world's most common animal. Total lunacy.

Yet Jeremiah prophesies it anyway. And he prophesies it with passion and excitement, sketching out for us what the new covenant will be like. I can picture him trying to explain what he can see, breathlessly describing it to his assistant: "Baruch, there's going to be a new covenant, not like the old one, but a new one, and the law won't be on tablets anymore, it'll kind of be in people's hearts and minds, and it will be so well-known that people won't even have to teach each other anymore, because everyone will know God, no matter who they are, because he'll forgive everyone's sins, in fact, he'll forgive them so utterly that he won't even remember them, and …" To Jeremiah's amazement, God was telling him about a covenant that would overwrite the one with Moses and deal with every aspect of Israel's sinfulness in a perfect and everlasting way.

It would be new, which meant it would replace the old one and make it obsolete, just as a new will overrides all previous ones. It would be written in people's hearts, which meant that God's people would not continually break it like they broke the last one; they would love to keep God's law, not just try to. It would be written in their minds as well, which meant that their thinking would be changed. It would restore a depth of relationship that had long since been damaged by persistent rebellion. It would be all-encompassing, so that everyone could know God. It would involve the total forgiveness and forgetfulness of all of their sins, not just the covering of them through the sacrificial system.

Now let's jump forward to another Jewish prophet who saw destruction coming and wept over Jerusalem. He is eating a meal with his friends, and as the meal comes to an end, something astonishing suddenly happens. After supper he takes the cup and announces, "This cup is the *new covenant* in my blood, which is poured out for you." We sometimes hear those words as a nice thing to say before communion. But if we understand the GodStory of the new covenant, like the disciples would have, it quickly becomes clear that Jesus is not just talking about the new covenant because he is going to the cross. He is going to the cross because he is starting the new covenant. After six centuries of waiting, the new covenant Jeremiah prophesied is here, the unbreakable one, in which the law will be written on men's hearts and the sins of Israel totally forgotten. As the writer to the Hebrews triumphantly puts it,

> Therefore [Christ] is the mediator of a new covenant, so that those who are called may receive the promised eternal inheritance, since a death has occurred that redeems them from the transgressions committed under the first covenant.... As it is, he has appeared once for all at the end of the ages to put away sin by the sacrifice of himself. (Heb. 9:15, 26)

You see, the old covenant was holy and good, but it dealt with sin in daily chunks. Every day, a priest had to do his duties and make sacrifices, which served as an ongoing reminder that Israel's sin had still not been fully dealt with. In the new one, by contrast, there was only ever one sacrifice—the "once for all" sacrifice of Jesus—and there has not been a single one needed since.

There never will be, either. This serves as decisive proof that sins have been completely wiped out, and that Jeremiah's new covenant has come about. Gospel preaching will never be the same again:

> *Our sufficiency is from God, who has made us competent to be ministers of a new covenant, not of the letter but of the Spirit. For the letter kills, but the Spirit gives life. (2 Cor. 3:5-6)*

THE STONE AND THE SON

*And in the days of those kings the God of heaven will
set up a kingdom that shall never be destroyed, nor
shall the kingdom be left to another people. It shall
break in pieces all these kingdoms and bring them
to an end, and it shall stand forever, just as you saw
that a stone was cut from a mountain by no human
hand, and that it broke in pieces the iron, the bronze,
the clay, the silver, and the gold. —Daniel 2:44–45*

Kingdoms come and kingdoms go. From God's viewpoint, it must
look ridiculous when earthly empires believe they will be there
forever; it is as if a group of aphids was to celebrate their eternal
dominance over a leaf. History is filled with kings who get too big
for their boots and are clobbered by Yahweh as a result—Pharaoh,
Sennacherib, Nebuchadnezzar, Herod—and when that happens, it
has one of two outcomes. Either the empire is destroyed altogether
(when did you last meet a Babylonian?), or it is left to another people
to rule over (Rome still exists, but it no longer governs Europe, and
the caesars are long gone). World history tells a consistent story: No
kingdoms last forever.

Which all makes the prophecy of Daniel 2 completely outrageous.
The next few centuries, Daniel says, are going to follow the normal
pattern of human history: The current world power (Babylon) will

be conquered by a new one (Persia), who will then be thrown down by a third (Greece), who will eventually be crushed by the military might of a fourth (Rome).[1] But during the rule of the fourth empire, the God of heaven will set up another one, which will never be destroyed, and which will never be left to another people—"it shall stand forever." That means it will be the only empire in history that neither gets wiped out nor passed to others. Bizarre.

That's not the only thing that is odd about Daniel's prophecy. It is rather strange wording, isn't it? "In the days of those kings" God will establish his kingdom. Normally, you only establish a kingdom by destroying the previous one. But Daniel doesn't say that. He says that God's empire will be set up while the other one is still there. It sounds like the everlasting kingdom is not going to be like any other, since it is going to exist while a worldly empire is still apparently in charge.

It is also outrageous that any of this should be prophesied by a Jew. The people of Israel didn't look like very likely candidates to receive an everlasting kingdom; as this prophecy was being written, they were not even in control of their own country, let alone anyone else's. Worse, they were not even *in* their own country, having been taken captive to Babylon by the very man Daniel is talking to. All in all, it sounds fairly ludicrous that Israel's God will set up an everlasting kingdom that will outlast all the others.

So why do we take it seriously? And why include it as a GodStory? Two reasons, really. For one, Daniel's track record at this point in the chapter is fairly impressive. Plenty of people in his day, and plenty in ours, made a living out of pretending they could tell people the meaning of dreams. Nebuchadnezzar's court was full of them, ancient

Mystic Megs who claimed they knew what dreams meant, so one day
he decided to call them on it. He declared that they had to tell him
not just what his dream meant, but what his dream was in the first
place—and that if they couldn't, they would be torn limb from limb.
You can imagine the panic: These horoscope writers were about to
get found out as frauds, so they told the king it was impossible, since
God does not dwell with flesh. Into this arena steps Daniel, who
promptly reveals that God does dwell with flesh, that he does reveal
mysteries, and that God knows both what the king dreamt and what
it meant. A random prophecy from an unknown person might not
carry much weight. But if you've just told the world's most powerful
man what he dreamt last night, under threat of death, you have the
right to be taken seriously.

The second reason for listening to Daniel is simpler: What he
prophesied came true. In the days of the fourth empire (the Romans),
the God of heaven did set up a kingdom, as we'll see a few narratives
later. That kingdom did begin while another empire appeared to be
in charge. It has, like the stone in Nebuchadnezzar's dream, broken
other kingdoms in pieces and crushed them. It has outlasted any
earthly kingdom, including the Romans. Two thousand years on,
it is still standing. And this empire continues to expand and fill the
earth, with new people groups being brought into it every year. You
probably know it as the kingdom of God.

This is a mind-blowing idea. The stone Daniel was talking about,
the kingdom of God, was not a question of Jewish soldiers conquering
foreign empires, but God's rule breaking in while those foreign empires
were still there and ultimately wiping them out altogether. This is how
Jesus explained what Daniel's stone was all about:

> *Have you never read in the Scriptures, "The* stone *that*
> *the builders rejected has become the cornerstone;*
> *this was the Lord's doing, and it is marvelous in*
> *our eyes"? Therefore I tell you,* the kingdom of
> God *will be taken away from you and given to a*
> *people producing its fruits. And the one who falls*
> *on this* stone *will be* broken to pieces; *and when it*
> *falls on anyone, it will crush him. (Matt. 21:42–44)*

That's pretty bold. Jesus is saying that his kingdom of preaching and healing and casting out demons is the stone that was rejected but will eventually break every worldly empire to pieces. Jesus is saying that his kingdom is the real fulfillment of Daniel 2.

But he's actually saying something even bolder than that, because this comes at the end of a parable about God sending his Son to Israel, and Israel rejecting and killing him. Now get this: In Hebrew, the word for "stone" (*eben*) sounds almost exactly like the word for "son" (*ben*). So Jesus is making a very provocative pun. Fundamentally, the rejected stone and the rejected son are one and the same: Jesus. Yet this rejected son, this rejected stone, is finally going to be vindicated. The Son is establishing an everlasting kingdom that will stand forever and crush all the others:

> *I saw in the night visions, and behold, with the*
> *clouds of heaven there came* one like a son of
> man, *and he came to the Ancient of Days and*
> *was presented before him. And to him was*
> *given dominion and glory and a kingdom, that*
> *all peoples, nations, and languages should serve*
> *him;* his dominion is an everlasting dominion,

which shall not pass away, and his kingdom one
that shall not be destroyed. *(Dan. 7:13–14)*

You know what? Daniel was right. The stone and the son are one
and the same.

Endnote

1. The New Testament makes it fairly clear that it is Rome, not Syria, who is the
fourth empire (in Daniel 2) and the fourth beast (in Daniel 7). References to Rome
as the "abomination of desolation" (compare Matthew 24 and Luke 21) are the most
obvious evidence; note too that Rome also conquered Greece with military force to
gain their empire (Dan. 2:40), whereas Syria inherited theirs, and that Rome could
be (and often has been) thought of as having conquered the known world, which
could certainly not be said of Syria in the second century BC.

THE SPIRIT POURED OUT

*And it shall come to pass afterward, that I will
pour out my Spirit on all flesh; your sons and
daughters shall prophesy, your old men shall dream
dreams, and your young men shall see visions.
Even on the male and female servants in those
days I will pour out my Spirit. —Joel 2:28-29*

Christians often stop the GodStory in the wrong place. Frequently, the gospel is talked about as creation—fall—crucifixion—resurrection—judgment, which involves jumping from Genesis 3 to Matthew 27 to Revelation 20, and skipping almost everything else. When people stop and think about it more carefully, they might include the life of Jesus (!) and perhaps even the history of Israel. In my limited experience, though, people almost always stop the tape at Easter Sunday and then fast-forward to the return of Jesus. This may be because people aren't too sure what happens in between or how relevant it all is to salvation. But in doing so, they miss one of the most thrilling bits, like a mountaineer so desperate to get home he fails to savor the summit. They miss the Spirit being poured out.

The prophet Joel wouldn't. Nor would Peter, who quoted Joel's words on the day of Pentecost in Acts 2, or Jesus, who spent most of his last hours talking about it (John 14—16). Luke would be astonished that anyone could talk about Christianity without mentioning the

Spirit and would explain in detail how Pentecost changed everything. Paul would go further and remind us that people without the Spirit didn't even belong to Christ (Rom. 8:9). To the apostles, and to Jesus, the pouring out of the Holy Spirit would represent one of the high points of the entire story; the bit that, quite literally, everybody was waiting for:

> *And behold, I am sending the promise of my Father upon you. But stay in the city until you are clothed with power from on high. (Luke 24:49)*

> *John baptized with water, but you will be baptized with the Holy Spirit not many days from now.... You will receive power when the Holy Spirit has come upon you, and you will be my witnesses in Jerusalem and in all Judea and Samaria, and to the end of the earth. (Acts 1:5, 8)*

> *This Jesus God raised up, and of that we all are witnesses. Being therefore exalted at the right hand of God, and having received from the Father the promise of the Holy Spirit, he has poured out this that you yourselves are seeing and hearing. (Acts 2:32–33)*

So what is so important about the pouring out of the Holy Spirit? Let me suggest five things.

First, he is the Spirit of power. This is probably the major emphasis of the GodStory in Luke through Acts. Jesus repeatedly promises power to his disciples, and Luke is then careful to show us that this has happened, with healings being done, wonders spoken, buildings shaken, demons cast out, and so on. When the Spirit was poured out, the age of power began, and that age continues—we can only accomplish God's mission if we are filled with God's power, just like a car can only run if it has been filled with fuel. The coming of the Spirit of power upon the church is one of the things Luke, and the early church he was describing, got most excited about.

Second, as we see in Jeremiah and Ezekiel, he is the Spirit of purity. There's a good reason he gets referred to as the "Holy" Spirit—he is the way unholy and impure people like us get to be holy and pure people like God. Galatians 5 is pretty blunt about this: If we walk in the Spirit, we will keep free from sin, because we have our very own live-in life coach showing us how to please God. Prophets with a passion for holiness, like Jeremiah and Ezekiel, were on the edge of their seats about the Spirit of purity coming to God's people.

Third, he is the Spirit of possession. This is especially significant for Paul; when the Holy Spirit comes upon us, we know we belong to Christ.[1] The Holy Spirit is the seal God puts on all believers, the proof in our hearts that we are his children, and the way we know that we are in Christ and Christ is in us. He is also the way that other people can know we belong to God; it was only when the Holy Spirit fell on Cornelius and his household that Peter was convinced they had been forgiven their sins and should be baptized, so the Spirit functions as a sort of ID badge for Christians, a bit like circumcision did for the Jews. When you have the Spirit, you know for sure you are God's possession.

Fourth, he is the Spirit of presence. Of all people in the New Testament, Jesus was the most insistent on this: It's for your good that I go away, he said, because when I do, I will send another helper to be with you (John 16:7). This didn't sound like good news when he first said it, but it was better than his disciples could possibly have imagined—because the helper he was sending was the Holy Spirit, the one who would bring God's presence to millions of believers at once. In an age of Wi-Fi, you won't find many people pining for a dial-up connection. In the same way, with the presence of Jesus available everywhere at once, Spirit-filled believers can do "even greater things" than he did.

Fifth, he is the Spirit of prophecy. Many Christians might be less comfortable with this than the previous four, but there's no getting away from it: It's what Joel was looking forward to in the passage we started with, and Peter and Paul were emphatic about it. When the Spirit comes, people prophesy. Not just prophets or experienced disciples, but sons and daughters, servants, Gentiles, young men. Prophecy happens frequently in Acts when people receive the Spirit, and Paul urges his most loony-fringe charismatic church, Corinth, to "eagerly desire" to prophesy.[2] No doubt some people have gone too far and made the use of certain gifts (like tongues or prophecy) the mark of salvation. But most churches I know face the opposite danger—that of being far too indifferent to the Spirit of prophecy, either by arguing he doesn't work like that now, or by reducing prophecy to teaching or preaching, or by simply not bothering to pursue prophetic revelation in their churches. It has been my privilege to interact with many gifted prophets in the last few years, and Joel was right. When the Spirit comes, people will prophesy. And he still does, so we still do.

The pouring out of the Spirit was quite something. Don't

stop the GodStory in the wrong place. Don't act as if Scripture jumps from resurrection to return and miss out on the marvel of the indwelling, empowering, baptizing, filling, gift-giving Spirit. The Spirit of Pentecost was the Spirit of promise—Joel's Spirit of prophecy and Jesus' Spirit of presence and Paul's Spirit of possession and Ezekiel's Spirit of purity and Luke's Spirit of power—all rolled into one glorious package and poured out in one glorious person. So, as Paul urges,

> *Do not get drunk with wine, for that is debauchery, but be filled with the Spirit, addressing one another in psalms and hymns and spiritual songs, singing and making melody to the Lord with all your heart, giving thanks always and for everything to God the Father in the name of the Lord Jesus Christ, submitting to one another out of reverence for Christ. (Eph. 5:18–21)*

Endnotes

1. Ephesians 1:13–14; Romans 8:14–17.
2. 1 Corinthians 14:1 (NIV).

For much of church history, there has been a lot of skepticism about the Spirit inspiring prophecy. Some of this has been for bad reasons (such as fear or poor theology), and some for good (a desire not to water down the authority of Scripture, for instance). But the result has been that many churches have become very nervous about pursuing prophecy, and many Christians are confused about how to desire prophetic revelation without making it equal to the Bible. These books, all written by recognized Bible teachers, may help you.

- *The Gift of Prophecy in the New Testament and Today* by Wayne Grudem

    This book is fairly academic, but it gives a thorough biblical explanation of the gift of prophecy in Scripture and why we can (and should) expect it today.

- *Surprised by the Voice of God* by Jack Deere

    An easier read, packed with powerful stories and biblical insights, Jack Deere's book also explains something of how the gift of prophecy should (and shouldn't!) be used. It is worth buying for the final chapter, "The Word and the Spirit together," alone.

- *Prophetic Evangelism* by Mark Stibbe

    Mark is an Anglican pastor and Bible teacher who has seen God speak wonderfully to unbelievers through his ministry. This book gives both biblical grounding and practical guidance for those who want to grow in prophetic evangelism.

• *The Holy Spirit and Spiritual Gifts* by Max Turner
    A world-renowned Bible scholar studies all the New Testament spiritual gifts, especially prophecy, in this very well-argued academic tome. Not for beginners, but an excellent resource.

ACT FOUR
JESUS AND RESCUE

CONCERNING HIS SON

*The gospel of God, which he promised beforehand
through his prophets in the holy Scriptures,
concerning his Son, who was descended from
David according to the flesh and was declared
to be the Son of God in power according to the
Spirit of holiness by his resurrection from the
dead, Jesus Christ our Lord. —Romans 1:1-4*

I don't think any verse in Scripture summarizes the gospel better than Romans 1:1–4. It is espresso theology, the gospel with not a word wasted, and it may therefore cause a splutter, or perhaps a head rush, to those of us who are used to drinking cappuccino or Americano. The Magna Carta contains over 4,000 words, and the Declaration of Independence, 1,321. Lincoln's Gettysburg Address, famously brief, was 267 words long. Rather more boringly, the European Union's directive on the sales of cabbages lasted an endless 26,253 words.[1] Yet here, Paul summarizes the greatest of all announcements in a mere 40 Greek words. Like espresso, it is enlivening and uplifting, but it is also very concentrated, so we're going to work through it carefully, sip by sip.

We are going to look later at the phrase "the gospel of God," so for now let's consider the fact that the gospel was "promised beforehand through his prophets in the holy Scriptures." The news that Paul is announcing, he says, is not, and never has been, a new thing. Christianity is the fulfillment of an old thing, the climax of thousands of promises and prophecies given through dozens of people across at least forty centuries. I don't know if you're into "whodunnits," but in a well-written mystery there is always a moment at the end when the detective explains how the murder was done and how all the puzzling strands you had been wondering about all come together in one solution. Paul is saying that the gospel is like that: the denouement, where all the puzzling strands you had been wondering about—exodus and exile, priests and sacrifices, kings and servants, suffering and victory—come together into one mind-blowing solution. That solution is the good news of God.

The sentence pivots on the next phrase, "concerning his Son." You cannot overstate the centrality of Jesus to the gospel. Ultimately, God's gospel is not "concerning his salvation" or "concerning his love," but concerning his Son. Remember, Paul is writing the opening sentence of a letter which is all about the gospel, and in which he is going to go into great detail about justification by faith, being in Christ, life in the Spirit, and so on. Paul is passionate about those things. But they in themselves are not what the gospel is about. They are like planets in orbit: large and important in themselves and with many smaller teachings built around them, but still revolving around a massive center of gravity far bigger than they are. In the middle of this theological solar system is the Son: his identity, his life, his death, his resurrection, and his reign. The gospel hinges on Jesus.

This thought is explored a bit further in the next two bits of the sentence. First, we read that Jesus was fully human: "descended from David according to the flesh." You might think this is a slightly peculiar thing to put in your summary of the gospel, but to Paul, Jesus' descent from David according to the flesh is hugely significant. It means at least three things. It means Jesus was a man, a real person who had a descent "according to the flesh," with real parents and ancestors. It means he was a Jewish man, a man who was circumcised and kept the law, and who could fulfill God's promises to Israel. And it means he was the rightful king, the heir of the throne of David, the one that the prophets had said would come and rule over the nations on behalf of Yahweh. The gospel is about a man.

Second, though, this man was "declared to be the Son of God in power." What a statement. This Jewish construction worker with a northern accent, who had brothers and sisters, who had a job and paid taxes and went to the toilet and slept and ate fish and cried and cracked jokes and washed feet, was declared to be the Son of God in power. If you've lost a sense of how shocking this is, just explain it to a Jew for a minute, and you'll quickly realize how controversial it originally was. This man from Nazareth was God's Messiah, described later as "God over all" (Rom. 9:5). The Son of God in power.

So how did this declaration happen? Paul says it happened "according to the Spirit of holiness by his resurrection from the dead." The third member of the Trinity finally joins the scene, as the Holy Spirit loudly announces to the world the authority now given to the Son, by his resurrection from the dead. Jesus was not raised by a medium, a séance, a Ouija board, or any other unclean spirit; he was raised according to the Spirit of holiness, in all his perfection and purity. The resurrection, fundamentally, was the Father's proclamation of the Son's lordship by the Spirit's power. If you worry that the Trinity is an impractical and theoretical idea, you just need to look at the empty tomb.

The result of all these things is summed up in the phrase "Jesus Christ our Lord." Again, you could write books on those four words, but the headline is that Jesus is the "Christ," the promised king of Israel; that he is "Lord," the ruler of the whole world; and that he is "our" Lord, the one whom *we* can know and praise and love and follow.

So the gospel is primarily a person, not an event. It's not "of Andrew, concerning his salvation"—which is hard to believe for those of us who think we are the center of the universe—but "of God, concerning his Son." When the early-morning papers come out with their front pages screaming, "Gospel of God!" and you search for the subtitle to tell you what the news is about, you get three simple words, accompanied by a picture of a Middle Eastern construction worker. They read, "Concerning his Son."

Endnote
1. I am grateful to John Hosier for this wonderful (and frightening) statistic.

THE KINGDOM OF GOD IS AT HAND

The time is fulfilled, and the kingdom of God is at hand; repent and believe in the gospel. —Mark 1:15

If you had asked Jesus to summarize the gospel of God, he would have said simply that the kingdom of God was at hand. If you had asked him what to do about it, he would have told you to repent and believe the gospel. If you had asked him what it meant, he would have showed you with his actions and told you story after story. Actually, for the three years he traveled around Galilee and Judea, that's pretty much all he did.

Many Christians have not been quite sure what to make of this. Removed from a Jewish context, and without any understanding of what "the kingdom of God" means, it is easy for modern Westerners to get confused. If you rummage through your New Testament, though, you'll find that not only did Jesus preach the kingdom in his earthly ministry, but he also spent the days after the resurrection explaining it; and the apostles followed his example, preaching and demonstrating it wherever they went. The fashionable claim that "Jesus preached the kingdom and the church preached Jesus" is, if you read the story carefully, complete rubbish. Both Jesus and the early church announced the same gospel—the kingdom of God is at hand—in word and action, with the life and death of Jesus firmly at the center. We may have since got muddled up about it, or dropped it altogether, but the apostles didn't. Neither did Jesus.

"The kingdom of God is at hand" is a climactic statement, the sort of statement that deserves to be announced with a loudspeaker or neon lights. Some statements are like that, and if they are written without an exclamation mark, they just look wrong: "Mildred just had triplets." "Which means the murderer was none other than ... Lord Bunfastley." "Look, the lost treasure of the Sierra Madre."[1] If comments like this are just dropped into conversation, it shows that the speaker has no idea what they mean. Like these, the announcement that the kingdom is at hand cannot be trivial; it brings to its conclusion centuries of waiting and has an immediate impact on the communities that hear it because they know the backstory.

So what does it mean? Well, the good news in the Old Testament, essentially, was that Israel's God was in charge, and all other gods, rulers, and nations were not. Faithful Jews knew that was true, but it often didn't look that way, because Israel (through its own sin) was frequently under the boot of a foreign power. So they looked forward to a day when all people would be able to see that Yahweh was in charge, as he returned to Jerusalem to destroy his enemies and bring restoration to his people:

> How beautiful upon the mountains are the feet of
> him who brings good news, who publishes peace,
> who brings good news of happiness, who publishes
> salvation, who says to Zion, "Your God reigns." The
> voice of your watchmen—they lift up their voice;
> together they sing for joy; for eye to eye they
> see the return of Yahweh to Zion. (Isa. 52:7–8)

"The kingdom of God is at hand," then, was a way of proclaiming that this was happening. After hundreds of years of waiting, Yahweh was coming back to his people, his enemies were going to be crushed, and his reign (which you could equally call his kingdom) was close by.

So far, so good. That was what the Jews meant, and that was what Jesus meant. The thing is, it quickly became clear that Jesus' idea of what these things looked like—the return of Yahweh, the crushing of God's enemies, and the breaking in of his reign—were not what any Jews were expecting. God's reign would not be accepted by everyone; in fact, lots of people (including the religious leaders) would reject it. The enemies that would be crushed included sickness, Satan, demonic powers, and sin, but not Roman soldiers. Worst of all, the return of Yahweh would mean judgment for Israel and her temple, not exaltation. The prophet from Nazareth was turning the popular notion of the kingdom of God on its head through the things he did and the stories he told.

Outsiders in Israel—lepers, deaf and blind people, those who couldn't walk, even the demonized—were being healed so that they could participate in the people of God. The "worst" sinners, such as crooked tax collectors and sexually immoral women, were being welcomed and invited to dinner. People with no place in Israel at all, such as Samaritans and Romans, were being included and, "worse," were held up as examples for good Jews to imitate. But Jesus knew what he was doing. He was signifying that the kingdom of God was much wider than anyone had realized and that it was going to incorporate more than just Israel.

And then there were the stories: sons who say they'll obey but then don't (like good Jews) will lose out to sons who say they won't obey but then do (like sinners). The son who comes back from the foreign pigsty gets invited to the banquet, while the son who has been there the whole time sits and sulks. You don't love just your Jewish neighbors, but everybody, even Samaritans. People who turn up at the vineyard late (like Gentiles) will get the same privileges as those who've been there all day (like Jews). God's banquet will be full of people you would never expect: outsiders, the poor, the sick, and unthinkables from the highways and hedges. The rich will be poor, the poor will be rich, the first will be last, and the last will be first. And so it goes on, as Jesus hammers a new understanding of the kingdom into his listeners. The kingdom of God is at hand, but it's not what you thought.

Of course, that picture of the kingdom flummoxed people. No one could figure out how Gentiles could ever be included in God's people without being made clean. No one could understand what healing and casting out demons had to do with anything. No one had any idea why God would want lepers and tax collectors and prostitutes in his empire. From this side of the cross, however, we have the privilege of seeing how the kingdom Jesus was talking about actually happens. We can see that God's rule is shown even more emphatically by saving Gentiles than by destroying them; we can see that Jesus had a plan to make even the most disgusting sinner right with God, whatever their race; and we can see that Yahweh is sovereign not just over politics, but over sickness, sin, Satan, demons, and even death. The kingdom of God is at hand—repent and believe the gospel.

Endnote
1. I owe these statements to playwright and comedian John Finnemore, in private correspondence.

REGENERATION

Now there was a man of the Pharisees named Nicodemus, a ruler of the Jews. This man came to Jesus by night and said to him, "Rabbi, we know that you are a teacher come from God, for no one can do these signs that you do unless God is with him." Jesus answered him, "Truly, truly, I say to you, unless one is born again he cannot see the kingdom of God." —John 3:1–3

I have always found it a bit peculiar when people ask if I am a "born-again" Christian. Is there another kind? It's like asking someone if they're a "medicine-dispensing" pharmacist or a "music-making" guitar player. The label "born-again" Christian implies that there are two sorts of disciple, those who are born again and those who aren't. But Jesus doesn't see it that way. He says that if you're not born again, you cannot see the kingdom at all.

It's an extraordinary statement. You can't go back inside your mother and go through the whole thing again, can you? It's a crazy idea. Yet there it is, on the lips of God himself. If you want to be in God's kingdom, you have to be "born again" (or, as theologians often say, "regenerated"). You have to be made from scratch by the Spirit of God.

The reason why Jesus says such a surprising thing is because he has a true understanding of human sinfulness and the size of the problem it presents. To many Jews like Nicodemus, the answer to the problem of human sin was obedience to God's law and faithfulness to his covenant. To Gentiles, human sin wasn't that much of a problem; their gods didn't require holiness from people, and most of their gods weren't even holy themselves. Jesus, however, knew that Gentiles had misunderstood God and that Jews had misunderstood people. He knew that there was a massive problem: God is holy, we are not, and no amount of effort would make up the difference. The solution was not to try again, or even to start again, but to be born again.

There's a great illustration of this in the cult sci-fi film *The Matrix*. The main character, Neo, has lived his life in a computer-generated dreamworld, in which everything looks and feels pretty much like the real world does today. In reality, however, he is permanently sitting in pink fluid along with millions of others, being harvested for electricity by a bunch of machines who have programmed his brain not to notice. To be released from his totally false dreamworld, he cannot think his way out of it or try his way out of it. The fake world he has been living in is too powerful. Instead, he has to be (almost literally) born again, removed from the pink fluid capsule and introduced to the real world for the first time. His muscles have to be built from the beginning, his worldview completely reconstructed, and his relationships totally transformed to adjust to the new, real world he now lives in. He finds it completely disorienting, and so do we. But being regenerated is the only way he can be saved out of falsehood and into reality.

That sort of radical remaking of people is what God gets up to through the gospel, by his Holy Spirit. We can't enter the kingdom without it, because the sinful nature we have been born with and the false worldview we have lived in for so long are very powerful. If sin was ultimately a problem with our thinking, we could solve it by thinking new thoughts; if it was ultimately a problem with our feelings, we could experience new emotions; if it was ultimately a problem with our actions, we could do new things. All other religions and secular worldviews that I am aware of believe that one of these three is the answer to humanity's problems. But they're all wrong. Sin is ultimately a problem with our being, our very nature, so it can only be solved by becoming a new creature. A totally new sort-of-something.

Which is what Jesus announces to a startled Nicodemus in the middle of the night. If you read Ezekiel 36, you'll see that it was not the first time anyone had said this; Jesus was proclaiming a reality that the prophets had talked about centuries previous. That doesn't mean it wasn't shocking, though. Hearing that your very being has to change to enter the kingdom, and that this only takes place by the power of God's Spirit, is a bit overwhelming. Yet it is also the foundation stone of the good news, because it means that we enter the kingdom on God's initiative and are given a completely new nature. Or, as Paul put it, "If anyone is in Christ, he is a new creation. The old has passed away; behold, the new has come" (2 Cor. 5:17).

This language of new creation is immensely powerful. Remember, in the beginning, God spoke light into being and there was light, shining in the darkness, brought about by the word of God through the Spirit of God (Gen. 1:1–3). Then, as John's gospel opens, we hear almost identical phrases being used to describe the new creation that starts with Jesus:

In the beginning *was the* Word.... *In him was
life, and that life was* the light *of men.* The
light shines in the darkness, *and the darkness
has not overcome it. (John 1:1, 4–5)*

If you're a disciple of Jesus, you're part of his completely new creation. You are not simply the "old you" who has learned to think, or feel, or act differently. You are a new creature, and you think and feel and act differently because of who you are. You have been regenerated, made new, born again by the Spirit of God.

CHRIST CRUCIFIED

For Jews demand signs and Greeks seek wisdom,
but we preach Christ crucified, a stumbling block
to Jews and folly to Gentiles, but to those who are
called, both Jews and Greeks, Christ the power of
God and the wisdom of God. —1 Corinthians 1:22–24

The cross of Jesus is a gory story of shame and pain, violence and silence. It is almost impossible to speak too strongly about it. If it doesn't bother us, then we probably haven't thought it through; like the Holocaust or the Rwandan genocide, it is the sort of event for which indifferent reactions are completely inappropriate. You can shrug your shoulders at Buddha, or even Muhammad, but as soon as you stop and think about Christ crucified, you cannot avoid a strong reaction. That's the whole point.

Extreme reactions to the cross take many forms. Many people think it's the dumbest thing they've ever heard, the idea that the suffering of a good man could be of any value whatsoever. These days, you will find lots of people get very angry with the cross, because it implies that their greed and sexual immorality and pride might require punishment. Still others will see it as one of history's great tragedies, as a good teacher gets cut down in his prime by the wicked powers-that-be. Some, wonderfully, will have their life turned upside down by the love and holiness they encounter there. One thing people do not do, however, is listen to the GodStory of Christ crucified and think nothing of it. Paul was right: Christ crucified is either notorious or glorious, but it can't be trivial. It's just too shocking.

So for the rest of this narrative, we're going to look very bluntly at what crucifixion is. This is not aimed to disgust you (although it will) or to overwhelm you (although it might), but to inform you, so that the phrase "Christ crucified" can have the same impact on you as it had in the first century. If you've seen *The Passion of the Christ*, you may know much of what follows, but reflecting on it again will probably not do you any harm. After all, as we have just read, Paul preached nothing else.[1]

Crucifixion was invented by the Persians somewhere around the fifth century BC, and it continued in widespread use until the emperor Constantine banned it in the fourth century AD. Widely acknowledged as the most despicable and disgusting way to kill someone ever devised, crucifixion has spawned its own word for intense pain (our word "ex*cruci*ating" literally means "from the cross"). In essence, it brought about slow death by asphyxiation, with victims gradually suffocating to death as their lungs filled with their own fluid. It could take days to die.

The criminal was secured to the cross by means of six-inch metal spikes driven through their wrists and ankles. In itself, this would of course bring about massive blood loss as veins and arteries were severed. The cross was then lifted vertically and rammed into a hole in the ground, at which point many bones would likely be dislocated. Hanging in the air with nothing but the nails supporting his weight, the criminal would have to push himself up and down in order to breathe (which is why, in the gospels, the bandits' legs were broken to make them die more quickly). At each point, the objective was to make crucifixion as long and torturous as it could be. So barbaric was the process that Roman citizens and women were hardly ever crucified—and if women were, they were nailed facing the cross, so that passersby could not see their suffering. Even the Romans knew how grotesque it was.

Crucifixion itself wasn't even the whole story. Before the cross, at least in Jesus' day, there was a severe penalty known as scourging, which involved being hung from a post in the courtyard while a multilashed whip, embedded with bone, glass, or metal, was used against the back, legs, and backside. A soldier would scourge in such a way as to ensure that the glass or metal got stuck in the criminal's flesh, and then rip it out, exposing the muscles and even bone. Some would die from the scourging alone, while those that survived were, unsurprisingly, physically unable to carry a splintered wooden stake uphill afterward. (In Jesus' case, all this unthinkable pain was compounded by a facial beating with a reed and a crown of twisted thorns.) Then, while hanging on the cross, naked and with the body in shock, the victim would typically lose control of his bodily functions, adding humiliation to his pain, and he would be ridiculed and spat upon by the gathered crowd. As urine, feces, blood, and sweat mingled together in a pool on the ground, the message of the cross could not be clearer: The Romans are in charge around here, and this "Messiah" is not.

All of which makes it quite staggering that within a few years, the event we've just studied had come to mean the exact opposite of that. According to Paul and thousands of people around the

Mediterranean world, the events of Good Friday meant the *Messiah* is in charge around here, and the *Romans* are not. That's the scandal, what Galatians 5:11 calls "the offense of the cross." It's also why people had such strong reactions to it. The Jews knew that people strung up on crosses were cursed by God, and the Gentiles knew that they were helpless criminals. So how could anyone not only admit their Messiah had been executed on a cross, but actively announce it? Put differently, how could anyone preach Christ crucified?

We'll see how and why in the rest of the GodStories in this part of the book. But for now, we need to understand why the cross was and is a stumbling block to Jews and folly to Gentiles. We need to recover our amazement at Calvary, our horror at what Jesus suffered, and our thankfulness for what he accomplished on our behalf. Most of all, we need to remind ourselves of the heart of our gospel: the proclamation of Christ crucified. It might be idiotic or infuriating to everyone else. But to those who are called, wherever we come from, it's the power of God and the wisdom of God.

Endnote

1. It is true that neither Paul nor the gospel writers ever described the specifics of crucifixion, except the reference to "scourging." But that is probably because crucifixion was so widely known that their readers already knew about them.

THE BLOOD OF JESUS

*You were ransomed from the futile ways inherited
from your forefathers, not with perishable
things such as silver or gold, but with the
precious blood of Christ, like that of a lamb
without blemish or spot. —1 Peter 1:18–19*

We left some questions hanging in the last narrative: How can the cross of Jesus be the gospel? How can something so gruesome as the torturous death of the Messiah be worth preaching? Does such horrible violence have to be part of the gospel? Well, in this narrative, we're going to try to answer some of these questions and hopefully establish that not only is the suffering of the cross a part of the gospel, but it's also the basis for it. According to the New Testament, the blood of Jesus isn't one extra component of the gospel, like a shot of vanilla in a coffee, without which the gospel would be a bit less good. It's like the coffee bean itself, the very heart and point of everything, without which the gospel wouldn't exist at all. The blood of Christ is essential.

We all hate blood. Some of us cope better with it than others, but there's something about its deep red color, its smell, its warm and sticky texture, that is a little bit nasty. So we avoid it. We are very careful to ensure we don't see our own blood, and if we do, we put a Band-Aid straight over it. Even though many of us eat meat regularly, we find the idea of physically spilling an animal's blood a bit disgusting. We hate the consequences of blood too: We wash our clothes if they ever get stained with it, and we shudder at scabs and hospital dramas. Blood carries life, and spilling it leads to death, so it makes us recoil, and we do what we can to get it as far away from us as possible.

That's how God feels about sin. He absolutely hates it. He recoils at its very sight and despises the color, the smell, and the texture of it. He hates what it is, and he hates what it does to people, to communities, and to creation. Just as we react strongly to blood, so God reacts strongly to sin; sin leads to death, so it makes him recoil, and he does what he can to get it as far away from him as possible.

You see, there is something quite deliberate about God's decision to make blood sacrifice necessary for the forgiveness of sins. He could have chosen anything—standing on tiptoes or running ten miles or juggling—but he chose shedding blood. And the reason for this is not that God is a sadist or a masochist who loves blood because he loves hurting people. (On the contrary, if you read your Bible, you'll see that all blood sacrifices take place because he loves *saving* people.) No, God chose shedding blood because he wanted us to feel the same way about sin that he does. He wanted us to see the link between sin, blood, and death, so we could understand the consequences of our sinful behavior.

This is graphically shown in the laws about sin offerings in Leviticus 4. If a normal person in Israel sinned and wanted forgiveness, they would have to bring a goat to the priest and kill it themselves. There is nothing sanitized about this; goats would have wriggled and squealed, and blood would have gone everywhere, leaving the

Israelite in no doubt that sin led to blood and thus to death. Then the priest would dip his finger in the blood and put it on the horns of the altar (which, if you're squeamish like me, is even worse). The whole sacrifice is deeply symbolic, designed to show that just as blood seeps out of a goat when you kill it, so life seeps out of a person when you sin. Sin is serious, God hates it, and so should we. Hence the shedding of blood.

But, and this is really important, this is not the main point of blood. God doesn't set up blood sacrifice so we can wallow in how terrible we are, or so he can remind us of our sins. He sets it up so he can *rescue* us from our sins. In Leviticus, animals shed their blood and died so that people didn't have to; once an animal had died on behalf of your sin, you couldn't be punished for it yourself, because the sin had been completely forgiven. In an even more powerful way, Jesus shed his blood and died so that we don't have to. We may feel as though our sins are so heinous that we deserve death—and they are, and we do. But the gruesome consequences of our sin, the death, and the blood spurting everywhere have already happened. To Jesus.

Rebecca Pippert tells the true story of a guilt-ridden woman who couldn't believe God could forgive her. She explained, through uncontrollable tears, that she and her husband had been youth workers in a church before they were married, and while going out, they had started sleeping together. She felt the guilt every time, knowing it was sinful in God's sight, but they still didn't stop. Then, while they were engaged, she discovered she was pregnant. Faced with an upcoming wedding, and certain that the church wouldn't be able to cope with the shame of her pregnancy, the couple made the most awful decision of their lives. They decided to have an abortion.

"My wedding day," she sobbed, "was the worst day of my entire life. Everyone in the church was smiling at me, thinking of me as a bride beaming in innocence. But all I could think to myself was, 'You're a murderer. I know what you are and so does God. You have murdered an innocent baby.' I know the Bible says that God forgives all of our sins, but I've confessed this sin a thousand times, and I still feel such shame and sorrow. How could I murder an innocent life?" At this point, Rebecca took a deep breath and said, "I don't know why you are so surprised. This isn't the first time your sin has led to death. It's the second."

That's the power of the blood of Jesus. It means that the thing you feel most guilty for—adultery, murder, pedophilia, or whatever—is actually only the second-worst thing you've ever done. Because of guilt, you may feel your sin deserves some sort of violent and unpleasant response. You're right. But the violent and unpleasant response, the smell and the texture and the spattering of redness, the blood and the death, have already taken place. And because they have, you are set free, "ransomed … with the precious blood of Christ."

THE THIRD DAY

*For I delivered to you as of first importance what
I also received: that Christ died for our sins in
accordance with the Scriptures, that he was buried,
that he was raised on the third day in accordance
with the Scriptures, and that he appeared to
Cephas, then to the twelve. —1 Corinthians 15:3–5*

If the GodStories had stopped on Good Friday, Christianity would be a tragedy. It certainly wouldn't be a gospel. If you pause at the end of Mark 15, you have the most depressing scenario imaginable: injustice done, a murderer released, the innocent killed, black skies, terrible pain, crying women, and a huge stone in front of the hero's tomb. At 6:00 p.m. on Friday evening, all our worst fears about the world have been confirmed. Jesus has fought death, and death has won. If Christ has not been raised, then Christianity is a false dawn, a rotten egg, a waste of time, and Christians are the most pitiful people on the face of the earth.

Thank God for the third day! You know the facts: A group of women go to perfume Jesus' body and find the stone moved and the tomb empty. Within a matter of hours, a number of people in several different locations have seen Jesus, alive and well, and the extraordinary explanation they give is that he has been resurrected from the dead. This is bizarre, because not only does the pagan world know resurrection is impossible, but the Jewish world knows it cannot possibly happen like this (resurrection, in Jewish thought, happens to everyone at once, at the end of the age). So announcing the resurrection seemed as ridiculous then as it does today. Yet the announcement spreads over the next few days, fueled by the growing witness list (at least five hundred by now, in a world where only two are required to establish something in court) and by the surprising failure of the authorities to produce the body. Within twenty years, news of the third day has reached Rome, and within thirty, the emperor has started burning Christians as streetlights to get them to shut up about it.

So that's what the third day was. Lots of modern people may not believe it, preferring instead some fanciful and often quite silly alternatives, but there it is anyway, the rationalist's riddle and the materialist's minefield. But what was the point of it? Why is the resurrection of Jesus a GodStory, rather than simply a set of GodFacts? What did the third day actually mean?

If you skim through your Old Testament, you'll find the third day was often important. You may, like me, have assumed the third day was just a statement of fact—Jesus was killed on day one, in the tomb on day two, and raised on day three. There is more to it than that, though, because Paul says Christ was raised on the third day "in accordance with the Scriptures." When Abraham went to sacrifice Isaac, it was on the third day that God provided a substitute so that he might live. At Mount Sinai, God appeared to the people on the third day, so powerfully that Moses had to warn people, "Be ready for the third day.... Whoever touches the mountain shall be put to death." Joshua (whose name in Greek would be Jesus, by the way) led the people of Israel into the Promised Land on the third day. Hosea prophesied that "on the third day he will raise us up, that we may live before him."[1] Substitutionary sacrifice, appearance in power, entry into the promises of God, and the awakening of Israel to new life all happened on the third day.

You see, the third day is full of meanings. Another very important meaning is that Jesus has been vindicated, or shown to be in the right. If Jesus had said all he said and done all he did, but remained in the tomb, it is unlikely we'd be reading about him, let alone worshipping him, for one simple reason: He would have lost. "Turn the other cheek" sounds great, but if it means you walk straight into excruciating death and stay there, I'll try something else. You say Yahweh is going to vindicate you and judge your enemies, but since you're still in a tomb, I'll take my chances, thanks. You might think you're the Messiah and you're bringing the kingdom of God, but, again, it doesn't look that way in Jerusalem on Saturday morning. But if, after saying all these things and doing all these things, Jesus was then raised from the dead by Yahweh himself—well, that makes everything sound a lot more credible, and it might even have changed the world. Perhaps I'd better listen to what he says about the kingdom of God.

Jesus' resurrection also means that God's new creation has started. Remember, in the Jewish world, the resurrection was something that happened at the end of the age, and it was part of God making all things new. The third day does not mean, as you might think from a number of songs and sermons, that Jesus has gone to heaven and we will too, leaving the earth to its sorry fate.[2] It means that the new age has already begun, life is overcoming death, and Jesus is the first phase of the complete renewal of everything (or, in Paul's phrase, the "firstfruits"). When the Rwandan genocide was happening, Western countries got preoccupied with airlifting out their citizens, when what was really needed was a heavyweight rescue operation to make peace, sort out the infrastructure, and renew the country. God isn't like that. He is not into airlifting Christians out of the world, but he is into a heavyweight rescue operation whereby he transforms the world through them. On the third day, this operation started.

The GodStory of the resurrection is absolutely glorious. It means Jesus was right, new creation has begun, sins are forgiven, death is defeated, we will be resurrected, and Satan is undone. It means Jesus fought death and Jesus won. The third day proves it.

Endnotes

1. Genesis 22:4; Exodus 19:11–12; Joshua 3:2 and following; Hosea 6:2.
2. This idea is tackled boldly and with characteristic clarity by Tom Wright, *Surprised by Hope* (London: SPCK, 2007).

COFFEE BREAK:

PAUSE AND PRAY

If you're anything like me, you may struggle to know exactly what to pray for other believers. I am fine praying for myself, and I can even pray for those who don't yet know the Lord, but what should I pray for Christians?

If you ever get stuck, you can always turn to the prayers of Paul and use them to pray for people you know. In this remarkable prayer from Ephesians 1, Paul thanks God and then asks that the church might understand something of the significance of Jesus' resurrection. It is a wonderful pastor's prayer: Father, let people get a bigger understanding of what you have accomplished in Jesus.

> *For this reason, because I have heard of your faith in the Lord Jesus and your love toward all the saints, I do not cease to give thanks for you, remembering you in my prayers, that the God of our Lord Jesus Christ, the Father of glory, may give you a spirit of wisdom and of revelation in the knowledge of him ...*
>
> *... having the eyes of your hearts enlightened, that you may know what is the hope to which he has called you, what are the riches of his glorious inheritance in the saints, and what is the immeasurable greatness of his power toward us who believe ...*
>
> *... according to the working of his great might that he worked in Christ when he raised him from the dead and seated him at his right hand in the heavenly places, far above all rule and authority and power and dominion, and above every name that is named, not only in this age but also in the one to come.*

And he put all things under his feet and gave him as head over all things to the church, which is his body, the fullness of him who fills all in all. (Eph. 1:15–23)

JESUS IS LORD

If you confess with your mouth that Jesus is Lord
and believe in your heart that God raised him from
the dead, you will be saved. —Romans 10:9

Paul's letter to the Romans is an underground political pamphlet. We tend to think of it as a theological essay, or the original Alpha course, and in some ways it is those things. But the bit we probably miss, largely because we don't live under the rule of the caesars, is the sharp political edge of the GodStory. Romans is dangerous, daring, and dramatic, largely because of the claim it makes about a Jew from Nazareth. If Jesus is Lord, then Caesar can't be.

To grasp the significance of this, we need to get ourselves into the Roman world of the first century. By the start of the first millennium, the Roman Empire stretched from Portugal to Israel, Germany to southern Egypt, and it was expanding all the time. This included a quarter of the world's population (and of course most in the empire had no idea that the other three-quarters were even there), so it was not long before Rome began to see itself, and particularly its emperor, as ruler of the world. The Greek word for this was *kurios*, which means "lord," and by the time of Jesus, Roman citizens were required to make a declaration of allegiance to the state: "Kurios Caesar," or "Caesar is Lord."

So when the early Christians started announcing that Jesus was risen and was Lord of the world, you can understand why it was dangerous. In saying so, the disciples were announcing that through his resurrection from the dead, Jesus had been declared the real ruler of the world, and Caesar was an impostor. The implications were clear: Loyalty should be pledged to Jesus and not to Rome. If Jesus tells you to preach or heal or plant churches, and Caesar tells you to shut up and stay put, you listen to the real Lord and ignore the fake one. It's high treason, so it might cost you your possessions or your life or your family, but confess it with your mouth anyway: Jesus is Lord, and Caesar is not.

That's just the start of it, though. Paul presumably subscribed to the theory that if you're going to put the fat in the fire, you might as well throw petrol on as well, so he fills his letter with sideswipes at Caesar. We know from archaeology that Roman emperors used to claim they were divine; coins were inscribed with the Latin words *divi filius*, "son of the divine." So Paul refers to Jesus as "the Son of God" in the very first sentence of this letter, using the exact Greek phrase that was used for Caesar. Roman emperors were often said to be gods after their deaths and declared to be worthy of worship and obedience. So Paul's political pamphlet announces that Jesus is God over all, that he alone is worthy of worship, that worshipping created beings is the essence of human sin, and that his job is to summon all the nations to obey the real Son of God. Caesar, seen as the bringer of peace throughout the empire because he conquered Rome's enemies, was frequently referred to as *soter*, or "savior." So Paul says that it is only by confessing the lordship of Jesus, the One who has truly brought peace and conquered your enemies, that you will be

saved. And this letter was written, of course, to Christians in Rome.
Imagine someone pinning a copy of *The Communist Manifesto* to the
Capitol Hill notice board in the 1950s, and you might get a sense of
how provocative this was.

There's more. In secular Greek, the word *euangelion*, which
means "gospel" and from which we get our word *evangelize*, was used
in two interesting ways. First, the birthday of the Emperor Augustus
was celebrated as *euangelion*: His birthday "signalled the beginning
of good news for the world."[1] Second, and more commonly, when
Caesar won a battle, heralds were sent back to "proclaim the good
news" (*euangelizo*). Paul, especially in Romans 10, seizes on the second
of these to announce that Jesus, the real Lord, has won the decisive
battle, and that all his disciples are now heralds bringing that news to
the world. The first was highlighted by his traveling companion Luke
in a provocative announcement that brings together a whole bunch
of Caesar phrases (roman type here) and applies them to Jesus:

> *Fear not, for behold,* I bring you good news
> *of great joy that will be for* all the people. *For*
> *unto you* is born this day *in the city of David a*
> Savior, *who is Christ* the Lord. *(Luke 2:10–11)*

It's no great surprise, knowing this, that Paul and his companions
were so often seen as political troublemakers. "These men who
have turned the world upside down have come here!" cried the
Thessalonians in Acts 17:6. "And they are all acting against the
decrees of Caesar, saying that there is another king, Jesus." There is.
That's the whole point. Jesus is Lord, and Caesar is not.

Let me make one point of clarification here, though. It could sound from all this like Caesar was the original lord, savior, and son of a god, and the early Christians stole these titles to make Jesus sound better. When you study the Old Testament, however, you realize that these titles go back way before Caesar and his empire, to the true Lord and Savior of whom Caesar was the parody and Jesus the exact imprint:

> *Come quickly to help me, O Lord*
> *my Savior. (Ps. 38:22 NIV)*

> *I, I am the Lord, and besides me*
> *there is no savior. (Isa. 43:11)*

> *Yet I will rejoice in Yahweh, I will be joyful*
> *in God my Savior. (Hab. 3:18 NIV)*

Jesus is Lord, and Caesar is not. Neither is the president or the prime minister or liberal democracy or academic learning or sexual fulfillment or tolerance or financial gain. Those things may be good, but ultimately they, just like Caesar, will be humbled before the throne of the One who made them, and all humanity will confess with their mouth, "Jesus is Lord!"

Endnote

1. From the Priene calendar inscription, cited in A. Deissman, *Light from the Ancient East*, trans., L. Strachan (London: Hodder and Stoughton, 1927), 366.

JUSTIFICATION BY FAITH

Therefore let it be known to you, brethren, that
through this Man is preached to you the forgiveness
of sins; and by Him everyone who believes is
justified from all things from which you could not be
justified by the law of Moses. —Acts 13:38–39 NKJV

Without justification by faith, "Jesus is Lord" might not be gospel at all. This sounds shocking, because the lordship of Jesus over everything is such wonderfully good news, but stop and think about it for a moment. In sixteenth-century England, the announcement that "Elizabeth is queen" was good news to lots of people, but it wasn't to the Duke of Norfolk or the Catholic clergy. The Normandy beach landings were celebrated by millions, but they were terrible news for the Nazis and their collaborators. In the same way, you would not expect the lordship of Jesus to be good news for people who had been opposing him. For everyone who collaborates with sin and rebels against their Creator, which amounts to every one of us, the lordship of Jesus ought to spell disaster.

Yet it doesn't. And the reason it doesn't is simple: justification by faith. This amazing truth—that rebels and collaborators like you and me can be made right with God by faith in his Son—means the lordship of Jesus spells salvation, not disaster. Lordship without justification would be terrifying news. Justification without lordship would be trivial news. But justification and lordship combined are tremendous news. It means we can be made right with the King of the universe.

Justification is a courtroom word. It describes the moment when the verdict is passed and the judge finds in your favor. Generally, we tend to think about justification as something that happens for defendants: I was innocently tried on the charge of murder, but I was not sent to prison, so I was "justified." However, justification involves not just being cleared of a crime (which is really being "acquitted") but also vindicated, shown to have been in the right, announced to be righteous. In many ways it is more like a plaintiff being awarded damages than a defendant being let off; more *Erin Brockovich* than *A Few Good Men*. And it happens to sinful people like you and me.

Why? How on earth can a just God look at you and me and not only let us off, but also declare us righteous? One answer kicking around first-century Judaism was that, although nobody was perfect, God justified people according to their faithfulness to his covenant and their obedience to the law of Moses. To Paul, however, this was appalling, since "if righteousness were through the law, then Christ died for no purpose."[1] As Paul concluded in the passage we started with, justification cannot happen through the law of Moses, but only through us being given the perfect obedience of Jesus as a gift. And the reason this is possible is that God has both condemned our sin (in Christ) and enabled our obedience (in the Holy Spirit). Thank God for the Trinity:

> There is therefore now no condemnation for those who
> are in Christ Jesus.... By sending his own Son in the

*likeness of sinful flesh and for sin, [God] condemned sin
in the flesh, in order that the righteous requirement of
the law might be fulfilled in us, who walk not according
to the flesh but according to the Spirit. (Rom. 8:1–4)*

Because our sin has been condemned in Christ and the righteous requirement of the law is fulfilled in us as we walk by the Spirit, it is completely just of God to justify sinners. Do you see? God does not say that because he is a nice guy he won't condemn us and he won't require us to fulfill the law. That would purchase our righteousness at the expense of God's righteousness. He says that because we are in Christ, *he has condemned us already*, and yet because we walk in the Spirit, *we will fulfill the law anyway*. In this mind-blowing demonstration of wisdom and teamwork from the Trinity, both sinful man (bolded below) and sinless God (roman type) are justified, vindicated, and declared to be in the right:

[People] **are justified by his grace** *as a gift, through
the redemption that is in Christ Jesus, whom God put
forward as a propitiation by his blood, to be received
by faith. This was* to show God's righteousness,
*because in his divine forbearance he had passed over
former sins. It was* to show his righteousness at the
present time, *so that* he might be just **and the justifier
of the one who has faith in Jesus.** *(Rom. 3:24–26)*

So that is the "why" of our justification. What about the "how"? How do we access this tremendous blessing of being declared righteous by God?

The answer given again and again in the New Testament is: by faith. Faith, not circumcision or law-keeping or any other observance, is the key that unlocks the privileges of justification, whether you are a Jew or a Gentile. But the word *faith* can, like *justification*, be misunderstood, so we need to be careful. There are two parts to it, and we may only think about one.

The commonly accepted part is that faith involves believing. The way our Bibles are translated, this is easy to see: *Faith* is the noun, and *believing* is the verb. If you don't believe that Jesus died, rose again, and was shown to be the Lord of the world and the Son of God in power, then you won't become his disciple. That's why preaching is necessary—people need to know something in their minds before they can believe it.

But the other part is that faith involves trusting. Trust doesn't simply mean the intellectual realization that someone exists, but the commitment of your life into their hands. When I teach this, I often bring someone to the front and ask them if they believe I am strong enough to catch them. They always say yes. I then get them to close their eyes and ask them if they will fall backward into my arms. Some falter at this point, but most give it a try. Finally, I get someone else to stand behind them and catch them, while I move well away. With my voice clearly coming from some distance away, I then ask the poor blindfolded person once again if they believe I will keep them safe. Not many take the plunge, but the ones that do show what Paul means by "faith": They trust me with their lives, even if they cannot understand how it will all work out.

That's the sort of faith Paul is talking about. That's the way in which we receive God's gift of justification. That's the way you and I, rebels and collaborators and sinners that we were, got made right with the Lord of the world. That's the GodStory of justification by faith.

Endnote

1. Galatians 2:21. For those who are horrified at this paragraph because they have been bamboozled by Ed Sanders, I recommend (in order) a quick read through Galatians, a pot of fresh coffee, and Stephen Westerholm's *Perspectives Old and New on Paul: The "Lutheran" Paul and His Critics* (Grand Rapids, MI: Eerdmans, 2004).

CHRISTUS VICTOR

He disarmed the rulers and authorities and
put them to open shame, by triumphing
over them in him. —Colossians 2:15

There's only ever been one victory. Literally. In all of history, there has only ever been one contest that you could look back to centuries later and agree it was won, permanently and definitively, by one side. Just one. In millions of attempts.

Think about the contenders. The Assyrians beat all their rivals in the eighth century BC but then lost to the Babylonians in the seventh, who lost to the Persians in the sixth, who got wiped out by the Greeks in the fourth, who crumbled in on themselves in the third, and so on. The Romans crushed all before them for four centuries, but they eventually lost too—just like the Goths, the Vikings, the Mongols, the Spanish, the British, and everybody since. IBM was dominant for a generation but then lost to Microsoft, who now look like they might well lose to Apple. England defeated all comers in the 2003 rugby World Cup and then lost to pretty much everyone. True victory—conquering rivals completely and permanently—is unheard of.

With one exception. In AD 30, a three-day campaign was waged by God against all of his most powerful enemies, sometimes referred

189

to as "rulers," "authorities," "principalities," and "powers." The main confrontation took place on a rubbish dump outside Jerusalem, where God, in his Son, Jesus, met Satan, sin, and death head-on. A mocking enemy was met by a defiant Son of God, and within six hours the one-sided battle was over, the victory triumphantly announced with the words "It is finished." On the third day, the victory parade began, as the risen Champion came out of the tomb to the amazement of earth and the applause of heaven. As Paul describes it in Colossians 2:15, God obliterated his enemies in Jesus, took away their armor, and made a public spectacle of them by parading their corpses through the streets.

The Latin phrase for this—although why theologians continue to use Latin words for this sort of thing is a mystery—is *Christus Victor*, which means "Christ the winner," or if you prefer, "the Conquering Messiah." You may remember the opening battle scene of *Gladiator*, where the Romans fight the Barbarian armies of Germania. It is far from an even contest, so vast is the might of Rome, but when the cavalry arrives, the Barbarians' fate is sealed, and as the camera pans around the dead bodies, a bloodied Russell Crowe raises high his sword and cries, "Roma Victor!" The cross was such a moment, only more so, because it still lasts today, sixteen centuries after the collapse of Rome. At Calvary, the stranglehold of sin was so smashed, and the dominion of death so decimated, that all those watching could do nothing but raise high their arms in triumph and cry, "Christus Victor! Christ has conquered!"

Strangely, considering how often this picture of the gospel appears in Scripture, it is not one that many of us are used to thinking about. In the West, we traditionally preach a gospel of individual forgiveness and a cross that saves us from the wrath of God. Such an explanation of Jesus' death, of course, is completely true, but there is more to the cross than that. It can be described not just in terms of the lawcourt, but in terms of the battlefield. We can worship God not just for his act of compassion, but for his act of conquest. And we can focus not just on what Jesus did to us (made us right with God), but on what he did to Satan, sin, and death itself (conquered them utterly). Such an understanding of the cross will not only keep us in line with the Bible, but it will also help us make sense of what Jesus is doing now. "For he must reign until he has put all his enemies under his feet" (1 Cor. 15:25).

We must be careful not to underplay the victory of Christ. Because we continue to live in a world where the rule of Jesus is not yet seen as it will be—a world where sin continues and sickness exists and people die—it is easy to live as if Colossians 2:15 were not true. We can think of the cross as God's opening gambit, the means by which we will defeat Satan rather than the means by which he already has been defeated. So everything in our lives, from our evangelism to our growth in personal holiness, becomes a question of completing a victory that has not yet been achieved. A widely used illustration of this idea presents the cross as like the D-day landings in 1944: The battle is not over, but the result is virtually assured, and all that remains is for us to press on until victory is complete.

That picture can be a helpful one, and I have used it myself in the past. But I think it underplays the picture of Christus Victor, Christ the winner. After all, the New Testament's theology of evangelism, let alone of sanctification, is not based on *completing* a victory but on *recognizing* one. Paul's exhortations to live holy lives in (for instance) Romans 6:15–23 and Ephesians 5:7–10 are not founded on completing Christ's victory over sin but on acknowledging it. And Peter's preaching of the gospel in Acts 2:32–36 is not about establishing Jesus' dominion over the nations but on announcing it.

As such, the gospel of Christus Victor means that our evangelism is less like defeating the last few battalions of the Axis army and more like proclaiming the end of the war to the last Japanese soldiers hidden in the Philippine jungle. You may have heard about Lt. Hiroo Onoda, who refused to believe that World War II was over and remained in hiding from 1945 until 1974, when he was finally reached by college dropout Norio Suzuki. He had lived under a false view of the world, pledging allegiance to a long-defeated power, for twenty-nine years. Suzuki proclaimed to him the good news that the war was over (another term for this is "preaching the gospel"), and Onoda finally brought his life and his behavior in line with the truth. That proclamation of the truth—that the war is over, that the enemy is defeated, and that all men can now live in the good of the victory of Jesus—is what evangelism is all about.

So if you feel the responsibility of establishing Christ's victory over darkness in the lives of your unbelieving friends, or if you are struggling with whether or not you will ever be able to overcome the ongoing power of sin in your own life, you need to lift your head and reflect for a while on Christus Victor, the only true winner in the whole of history. In other words:

> Weep no more; behold, the Lion of the tribe of
> Judah, the Root of David, has conquered. (Rev. 5:5)

On Facebook, my friend Andy Chevalier lists his religious views as "Jesus wins." This is the essence of Christus Victor, really, and it's a wonderful way of summarizing Christianity. To help us get it into our spirits, I've done something slightly different this time and given a few resources that engage more with our hearts than with our minds. They may help you connect with how much, and how powerfully, Jesus has won.

"Everything" by Lifehouse

There's a tremendously powerful drama online about the victory of Christ. It still brings me to tears, and I have seen hundreds of people respond to the gospel after seeing it. Just type "Lifehouse Everything Drama" into YouTube, and it will appear. Jesus wins!

"That's My King" by Dr. S. M. Lockridge

Many people have now come across the wonderful words spoken by Baptist pastor S. M. Lockridge, but they have now been put into a strong audiovisual presentation which is available to view on YouTube, and can be downloaded from Igniter Media. It will stir your heart as you remember who Jesus really is.

"All Hail the Lamb" by Dave Bilbrough

This widely sung chorus is a wonderfully simple statement of the victory of Jesus and its consequences.

"The Power of the Cross" by Stuart Townend and Keith Getty
One of the best hymns of recent years, this focuses both on the suffering and the triumph of the cross. The final two verses are wonderfully profound and uplifting.

Christ's Glorious Achievements **by Charles H. Spurgeon**
This series of sermons is practically an exposition of the phrase "Christus Victor," and there is no one better than the prince of preachers to explain it.

THE CUP
. . . .

*And he withdrew from them about a stone's throw,
and knelt down and prayed, saying, "Father, if you
are willing, remove this cup from me. Nevertheless,
not my will, but yours, be done." And there appeared
to him an angel from heaven, strengthening him.
And being in an agony he prayed more earnestly;
and his sweat became like great drops of blood
falling down to the ground. —Luke 22:41–44*

We deserve a cup, and not in a good way. Today, the word *cup* suggests either a drink or perhaps a trophy, both of which are positive. In Scripture, however, it often has an ominous note and is the image most often used to describe the wrath of Yahweh. So the fact that we deserve to drink it is bad news. Very bad news.

A quick word study will make the point. In the Old Testament, although there are one or two exceptions, the cup image is usually used of Yahweh's wrath, which those who sin against him have to drink. If we are to have any idea what Jesus was talking about in the prayer we have just read, then we need to understand this:

*Thus Yahweh, the God of Israel, said to me: "Take from
my hand this cup of the wine of wrath, and make all
the nations to whom I send you drink it. They shall*

*drink and stagger and be crazed because of the
sword that I am sending among them." (Jer. 25:15–16)*

*A cup of horror and desolation, the cup of your
sister Samaria; you shall drink it and drain it out, and
gnaw its shards, and tear your breasts; for I have
spoken, declares the Lord Yahweh. (Ezek. 23:33–34)*

These are graphic and violent images, and they make us cringe by their bluntness, but they are like that to communicate the sheer anger that God feels at sin. Imagine how you would feel about a snake that had slid into the crib when you weren't looking and killed your baby, and you might get a sense of the feeling sin provokes in Yahweh. Now, just in case you want to jump into the New Testament to make this image go away, the wrath imagery is even clearer there, with every single metaphorical use of "cup" referring to suffering and/or wrath.[1] By Revelation, the picture has become terrifying indeed, with phrases like "the cup of the wine of the fury of his wrath" (16:19). Scary.

This wrath exists because of my sin and yours. It is easy to think of wrath being poured out for extreme things others do, like genocide and child abuse, but harder to see that it is also poured out for more everyday things that we do, like greed, lust, lying, and idolatry—basically, our refusal to obey God at all times. Romans 2:5 says that it is "because of your hard and impenitent heart you are storing up wrath for yourself," which is frightening, because it means my stubborn attitude toward God causes a cup of wrath to be filled somewhere and kept in storage for the day of judgment. At some point, someone is going to have to drink it.

A fresh illustration might show how dreadful this is. Imagine all the waste you had ever generated in your life was stored in a giant septic tank. Litter, Coke cans, wood chips, uneaten food, vomit, excrement—all in a huge, stench-ridden vat. Then, at the end of your life, you were told the entire tank was going to be poured over your head. That is the position we are in with regard to the wrath of God: All our waste, sin, greed, and pride have been storing up God's anger. On the day of judgment, that septic vat is going to be poured onto our heads.

Except that it isn't. That is the wonder of what Christ accomplished. Faced with an enormous vat of God's righteous wrath that was due to be poured out over our heads, Jesus took our place and received the punishment instead. At Calvary, the septic tank of judgment was emptied over Jesus' head instead of ours, until every last drop of sludge was gone. The cup of God's fury was downed in One, once for all.

Hence Gethsemane. With the horror of the cross approaching, Jesus knows what is about to happen. He is peering into the cup of wrath, physical agony combined with a spiritual separation from the fellowship of the Trinity. He is looking into the cup of sin, the perfectly holy one confronting the reality of bearing all that sin upon himself and having it condemned in his flesh (Rom. 8:3). He can see the aloneness, too; no matter how we feel, none of us is ever truly alone—we have some family or friends we can call and a relationship with God—but Jesus, abandoned and strung up, mocked by earth and forsaken by heaven, was absolutely alone. The terrible experience looming, he cries out in anguish, "Father, if you are willing, remove this cup from me," and his sweat is like drops of blood falling to the ground. "Yet," he prays in astounding obedience, "not my will, but yours, be done."

In that moment of submission, and in the twelve hours that followed, the cup of God's anger was drained altogether for those who believe. It now stands empty. Even if as a Christian you wanted to drink it, there is nothing left; the hero of Gethsemane has cleared it completely. The massive septic tank of wrath at my pollution and slime, my sin and rebellion, has been completely poured out on Jesus, so that even if I stood under the vat myself, there would be nothing in it to fall on me. Because Jesus accepted the cup on my behalf, it is actually part of God's justice that I don't have to (1 John 1:9). There is no punishment left. It has all been taken.

Next time you share the Lord's Supper, consider the cup. Remember that Jesus had to drink your cup to enable you to drink his. And do it in remembrance of him.

Endnote

1. The metaphorical uses of *poterion* ("cup") are: Matthew 20:22, 23; 26:39; Mark 10:38, 39; 14:36; Luke 22:42; John 18:11; Revelation 14:10; 16:19; 17:4; 18:6.

EVERYONE WHO CALLS

For there is no distinction between Jew and Greek;
the same Lord is Lord of all, bestowing his riches on
all who call on him. For "everyone who calls on the
name of the Lord will be saved." —Romans 10:12–13

When I was a child, I used to be terrified of calling people on the phone. It was awful. I would really want to go round to a friend's house, but my parents would tell me that I could only go if I rang them myself and asked, so I wouldn't go. On one occasion, I left behind something really valuable, but because I was too scared to phone them and ask for it back, I lost it forever. Calling can be difficult.

For me it's a pride thing, and it probably predates the telephone. That phenomenon has been around throughout history: Calling on someone's name, whether by phone or in person, means making yourself vulnerable, asking them for help, and knowing that it is entirely in their power to accept or decline. So it requires humility, an acknowledgment of need.

It is exactly that humility, that acknowledgment of need, that we find in Scripture when people call on the name of the Lord. It is the earliest expression of worship to Yahweh, going back to Genesis 4:26, and appears a number of times in the Old Testament as people ask God for things and then thank him for things. David puts it simply:

> Give ear, O Yahweh, to my prayer; listen to my
> plea for grace. In the day of my trouble I call
> upon you, for you answer me. (Ps. 86:6–7)

This sort of thinking, while it sounds very easy, is actually very humbling. For the king of Israel to admit that he can do nothing to get himself out of his trouble, but needs to call on the name of Yahweh to help him, requires an honest and unflattering view of his own abilities.

It is not surprising, then, that Paul says those who call on the name of the Lord will be saved. We would expect that, wouldn't we? If people are to get saved by God, whatever that means, they need to understand their position, believe that he is able to help, and call on him to save them (just as a man in a burning building needs to understand his position, believe that firefighters are able to help, and call on them to save him). And because God is loving and gracious, whenever his people call on his name, he runs to their rescue. So far, so good.

But Paul is saying much more than that, and it is very radical. He is saying that *everyone* who calls on the name of the Lord, irrespective of their Jewishness (or lack of it), will be saved. That sort of talk puts the cat among the pigeons. It is all very well to say that God's people get saved by calling out to him for help, but to say that the Gentiles can do this too, with no descent from Abraham, no law, no land, no temple, and no history of following Yahweh whatsoever—that is a remarkable statement. But Paul is insistent. There is no distinction between Jew and Greek. Salvation is for everyone who calls in faith.

The Jews were like people with breakdown insurance. Like members of the AA (in the United Kingdom) or AAA (in the United States), they were members of a group that had certain privileges associated with it, one of which was the right to be rescued when they got into trouble. Because of their membership in this group, they could call on the name of their rescuer any time, day or night, and he would come to their aid, whether in Egypt, Babylon, or on the edge of the M25.[1] But calling takes humility, and it takes faith. And a number of Jews had stopped calling, either because they didn't realize they needed saving, or because they didn't believe God would do anything about it. Stranded on the edge of the M25, with smoke pouring from the head gasket, many Jews had a phone and a membership card but never called for help to the one who could save, so they were left by the side of the motorway. As Romans 9:32 shows, being a member of the group doesn't help you if you never call in faith.

You see, what really counts is calling in faith, not membership in the group. And therefore, Paul argues in a wonderful piece of God-inspired logic, *even people who are not members of the group* can get rescued if they call in faith. This happened to my wife, Rachel, recently. She broke down with a dramatic shudder on the M25, in the dark, in rush hour. Having barely reached the hard shoulder, she was in significant danger but was not a member of the AA, so she had no right to call for rescue. But she had read Romans 10. She knew that if she called upon the name of the AA in her day of trouble, in humility and in faith, she could become a member over the phone, and they would come to her rescue. Within half an hour, amazingly, she had joined a group she had never been part of, received all its privileges, and been saved in her time of need. Simply by calling on their name. Just like the Gentiles.

You see, it doesn't matter whether you were born into the group. It doesn't matter whether your parents were members. In fact, there is no distinction whatsoever between members and nonmembers, for the same Lord is Lord of all, and he pours riches on anyone who calls. All that matters is whether you called, in humility and in faith, on the name of the One who is able to rescue you. For everyone who calls on the name of the Lord will be saved.

Endnote
1. For the benefit of my international readers, this is London's orbital motorway.

THE END OF THE LAW

*For Christ is the end of the law for righteousness
to everyone who believes. —Romans 10:4*

Three-letter words can be deceptive. They look very simple, and you think you know what they mean, but there often turns out to be a lot more to them than meets the eye. The English word *set*, for instance, is very simple—every four-year-old in the country would know it and be able to use it in a sentence—yet my *Guinness Book of Records* informs me that it has 128 meanings as a noun and 56 as a verb. Three-letter words can sometimes be more wide-ranging than we might think.

The word *end* is like this in the Bible. At one level, it is very obvious what it means, but at another, its meaning is far richer than it first appears. This is because the Greek word *telos*, which we translate as "end," has at least two clear meanings. It can mean simply the termination of something, as in "the end of the century." But it can also mean the purpose of something, as in "the chief end of government." In fact, when Paul said that Christ is "the end of the law," he probably meant both.

Take the simpler one first. In Christ, Paul says, the law is finished. All of it. The ceremonial law no longer marks off the people of God from everyone else, because new boundary markers, like water baptism and the Holy Spirit, have replaced the old ones (which is why the Jewish food and purity laws, not to mention circumcision, were not imposed on Gentile disciples). The sacrificial law no longer provides access to God, because Christ's sacrifice has secured forgiveness for all who trust in him. More surprisingly, the moral law no longer acts as our final authority on behavior, because we serve in the new life of the Spirit, not under the old written code (Rom. 7:6). In every way imaginable, the era of Torah government is over.

So the announcement that Christ is the end of the law, for righteousness to everyone who believes, is amazing news. It means that I am no longer under condemnation, because I have been set free from the law of sin and death. As a Gentile, it means even more than that: It means that I can be part of the people of God on an equal footing with Jewish disciples. In short, the end of the law means that there may be righteousness for everyone who believes. Which includes me.

So how does this fit with Jesus' statement that not an iota or a dot will disappear from the law until heaven and earth pass away (Matt. 5:18)? If the law has finished, hasn't Jesus' prophecy been proved untrue? Well, this is where the second meaning of *end* comes in. You see, in Christ, the law is not just finished, it is fulfilled. Christ is the purpose of the law: He is its explanation and its goal. The law, exposing sin for what it is, points forward to Jesus as the only way in which it can be kept. And because Christ fulfilled the law perfectly, we who are in Christ have fulfilled it as well.

I love sailing in lakes and on the open sea. But I used to hate the training sessions. The instructors would walk around you, barking instructions at you and making you tack, over and over again. They would drum the procedures into you: Change hands, say "ready about," duck, push the rudder away from you, change sides, adjust the jib. And they would remind you that no matter how good a sailor you became, you would always need to do these things; that not an iota or a dot of their procedures would disappear until the wind stopped blowing, if you like. Because I wasn't very talented, I kept getting it wrong and ended up either banging my head or capsizing the boat. I could not fulfill their instructions.

But my brother could. When he and I sailed together, he took the helm, and he had the procedures down to a fine art. In fact, he was so good that I never even had to worry about them—simply by being in his boat, I fulfilled all the instructors' commands without even thinking. I still had a responsibility to trust him and not to get in the way of what he was doing, but in every other way I relied on his performance, not mine. David was the end of the procedures for me, not because the procedures were no longer valid, but because he had fulfilled them perfectly on my behalf.

In the same way, Christ is the end of the law, not because it was inadequate but because we were. He did not come to abolish it but to fulfill it, and in the process he demonstrated its goodness far more than we ever could have. As Spurgeon argued,

> I venture to say that if the whole human race
> had kept the law of God and not one of them
> had violated it, the law would not stand in so
> splendid a position of honor as it does today ...
> God himself, incarnate, has in his life, and yet more
> in his death, revealed the supremacy of law; he
> has shown that not even love nor sovereignty can

set aside justice. Who shall say a word against the
law to which the Lawgiver himself submits?[1]

What a truth: that Christ became the end of the law, not by ignoring it or abandoning it for being too difficult, but by submitting to it perfectly, fulfilling it, and then allowing us to fulfill it in him. The law is not only finished, but it is also fulfilled. Christ was not just its cessation, but its culmination, completion, and climax. For Christ is the end of the law, for righteousness to everyone who believes!

Endnote

1. Charles Spurgeon, "Christ the End of the Law," in *Christ's Glorious Achievements* (Tain, UK: Christian Focus, 2003), 21.

RECONCILIATION

All this is from God, who through Christ reconciled
us to himself and gave us the ministry of
reconciliation; that is, in Christ God was reconciling
the world to himself, not counting their trespasses
against them, and entrusting to us the message
of reconciliation. —2 Corinthians 5:18–19

There are two types of reconciliation in the world, and you can't have the second one without the first. The first type is vertical: peace with God. The second type is horizontal: peace with other people. And you can't have anything approaching true peace with people unless you have peace with God. I don't mean peace as the absence of war, because that is achieved all the time, on and off. I mean peace as the Bible has it—*shalom*, wholeness, completion, welfare, safety. That sort of reconciliation with people is impossible unless you have first been reconciled to God.

Evidence is everywhere. Stopping a war doesn't necessarily produce peace, any more than stopping an affair necessarily produces a healthy marriage. You can stop people fighting, but they will still hate one another; UN "peacekeepers" are usually nothing of the sort. You can even stop people speaking against those of other races and cultures (as happens in much of the West), but it doesn't reconcile them—they still dislike Muslims or asylum seekers or middle-class people or gypsies or evangelicals. The only way to reconcile people to one another is to reconcile them to God first: black and white, rich and poor, slave and free, Jew and Gentile. That is why the church is such a great idea and why mixed-race congregations in places like Johannesburg and Jerusalem and Jackson, Mississippi, are so powerful. It is also why fighting racism without the gospel is ultimately ineffective.

Let's think about an illustration of the importance of being reconciled to the major things (like God) before we can sort out the minor. Pouring coffee while riding on a train is achievable. It is difficult, but it is achievable. Obviously, you are never quite sure if the train is going to jolt, so you have to stand as stably as possible, keep your eye on the cup at all times, and have a very steady hand. And if you lose concentration, or if the train bumps on a rail, then you will quickly have an irate customer with first-degree burns and coffee-stained trousers. But if you concentrate, and if the rails are smooth, you will probably be all right. Reconciling the coffee with the cup is tricky but possible.

If the train comes off the track, however, it is a very different story. Suddenly it becomes absolutely impossible, and very dangerous, to try and pour coffee. The trolley, the urn, and the steward are sent flying around the carriage, and everybody dives for cover; you would never see a steward trying to pour coffee at such a time, because it would be such a ridiculous choice of priorities. From the second the train leaves the track, reconciling the coffee with the cup becomes completely unimportant to him. He is just hoping the train will get reconciled with the rails.

We live in a world that, through our own sin and bad stewardship, has come off the rails. It is shuddering violently, creating chaos where there was meant to be order, and bringing conflict where there should be peace. In consequence, everybody within it is in turmoil and strife, whether racially, environmentally, socially, or economically. All of us need desperately to be reconciled to one another. Yet this "ministry of reconciliation" will go nowhere until the world is back with God, just as the coffee will go everywhere until the carriage is back on the rails. We need peace with God even more than we need peace with each other.

What an amazing announcement, then, is 2 Corinthians 5:19 that "in Christ God was reconciling the world to himself, not counting their trespasses against them, and entrusting to us the message of reconciliation." In Christ, Paul says, God was putting the train back on the rails. In Christ, God was bringing about the *shalom* we really needed, peace with our Creator, so that the message of reconciliation could be proclaimed. In Christ, God was solving the peace problem at the macro level, and now all the micro-level peace problems like racism, economic inequality, class war, and hatred can be solved as well.

At the center of this reconciliation message is the cross. It was the cross of Jesus Christ, where the reason for our fractured relationship was dealt with, that brought humans and God back together again and laid the foundation for human and human to be brought back together again. Look at the sweeping language of total reconciliation Paul uses in Ephesians:

> *For he himself is* our peace, *who has* made us both
> one *and has* broken down in his flesh the dividing wall

of hostility *by abolishing the law of commandments
and ordinances, that he might create in himself* one
new man *in place of the two,* so making peace, *and
might* reconcile *us both to God in one body through
the cross, thereby* killing the hostility. *And he came
and preached* peace to you *who were far off and*
peace to those *who were near. (Eph. 2:14–17)*

The cross means that we can be at peace with our Creator, and therefore that we can be at peace with one another. And "all this is from God, who through Christ reconciled us to himself."

That's what I call reconciliation.

COFFEE BREAK:

When we read short announcements of the gospel, it is good to absorb the broader context in which they appear. If we don't, we run the risk of misinterpreting the text, and we also lose much of its power. Second Corinthians 5 is a great example, because it links together our peace (reconciliation) with the basis for it (becoming the righteousness of God) and with our mission (calling others to find peace with God). Meditate on each verse of this wonderful passage, and see how much you can commit to memory.

> *For the love of Christ controls us, because we have concluded this: that one has died for all, therefore all have died; and he died for all, that those who live might no longer live for themselves but for him who for their sake died and was raised.*

> *From now on, therefore, we regard no one according to the flesh. Even though we once regarded Christ according to the flesh, we regard him thus no longer. Therefore, if anyone is in Christ, he is a new creation. The old has passed away; behold, the new has come.*

> *All this is from God, who through Christ reconciled us to himself and gave us the ministry of reconciliation; that is, in Christ God was reconciling the world to himself, not counting their trespasses against them, and entrusting to us the message of reconciliation.*

> *Therefore, we are ambassadors for Christ, God making his appeal through us. We implore you on behalf of Christ, be reconciled to God. For our sake*

211

*he made him to be sin who knew no sin, so that in
him we might become the righteousness of God.*

*Working together with him, then, we appeal to
you not to receive the grace of God in vain. For
he says, "In a favorable time I listened to you,
and in a day of salvation I have helped you."
Behold, now is the favorable time; behold, now
is the day of salvation. (2 Cor. 5:14—6:2)*

IMPUTED RIGHTEOUSNESS

*For what does the Scripture say? "Now Abraham
believed God, and it was imputed to him as
righteousness." Now to the person who works,
the reward is not imputed to him according to
grace, but according to debt. But to the person
who does not work, but believes in the justifier of
the ungodly, his faith is imputed as righteousness.*
—Romans 4:3–5, author's translation

In 1992, Rick Hoyt completed the Boston Marathon in two hours
and forty minutes. There might not seem anything remarkable about
that, but Rick was strangled by his umbilical cord at birth and ever
since has been unable to control his limbs. He cannot talk or feed
himself, let alone walk, so the fact that he has completed a marathon
just thirty-five minutes shy of the world record is somewhat surprising.
Because of Rick's love of sport, however, his father has pushed him,
carried him, and towed him for a thousand marathons and fun
runs, numerous triathlons, cross-country skiing, rock climbing, and
even a 3,700-mile cycle ride across the USA. Rick cannot move. He
certainly cannot run or swim. All he brings to the table is a love for
sport and a reliance on his dad. Yet, as of 2007, he is credited with
completing 212 triathlons, simply by sitting there and trusting the
one who is pushing him. His faith in his father means he ends up

being rewarded without doing any work whatsoever. Like Abraham.

Rather more mundanely, I tend to infuriate my wife, Rachel, by double-booking myself for things. I frequently forget to tell her about something I've arranged, and that means we get lots of clashes, so recently she came up with a rule: If I don't write something on our calendar, I am not allowed to do it. It's a good rule, because it means it's my problem if I am disorganized. But the other day, I had a trip away with friends that I really wanted to go on, and I forgot to write it on the calendar. Disaster. All I could do was grovel and apologize, and ask her to forgive me. Fortunately, in a wonderful demonstration of grace, Rachel wrote it on the calendar for me and allowed me to go. My apology was imputed (or reckoned or credited or counted) to me as a calendar entry.

Abraham knows how I feel. About four thousand years ago, he believed an outrageous promise of God that he and his barren wife would have countless children who would inherit the world, and his belief, his faith, was reckoned to him as righteousness (Gen. 15:6). Note that phrase. It is accounting language: Because of Abraham's faith, God chose to make an entry in the "righteousness" column that "reckoned" or "imputed" him righteous even though he wasn't at the time.[1] Remember, Abraham at the time was "ungodly." There was nothing in his faith that made him righteous before God, but somehow, in the divine economy, Abraham's trust in Yahweh was imputed to him as righteousness.

Today, this idea of undeserved, imputed righteousness is controversial in some circles, but it really shouldn't be. For a start, the whole argument of Romans 4 is that we are counted righteous in the same way Abraham was, and Abraham's righteousness was credited to him on the basis of faith (a point Paul also makes in Galatians 3:1–9). Not only that, but Paul then uses a bookkeeping illustration about wages to make the point clearer. If you work for somebody, then you don't get paid out of grace, but out of debt.

Think about it. If you work hard all month, then your paycheck is not a gift from your employer, is it? But if, like Rick Hoyt, you had done no work at all and simply trusted in somebody else's work on your behalf, then you would not deserve to be paid. So any payment you received would be a gift, on the basis of your trust in someone else. Your reward would be imputed to you, if you like, through faith.

That is how you and I get righteousness imputed to us by God. We are justified when we are ungodly, not when we are good; we are justified as a free gift, not as a reward for our efforts. Our righteousness is not a hard-earned paycheck from God for all our goodness and hard work. It is a gift, plain and simple, imputed to us on the basis of faith. We bring nothing to our salvation, simply trusting that our Father is strong enough and loving enough to take us with him to victory. And because of that trust, that faith in the One who justifies the ungodly and the undeserving and the uncircumcised, we get a righteousness that is not our own imputed to us from somewhere else. For free. Just like Abraham.

> But the words "it was counted to him" were not written for [Abraham's] sake alone, but for ours also. It will be counted to us who believe in him who raised from the dead Jesus our Lord, who was delivered up for our trespasses and raised for our justification. (Rom. 4:23–25)

Endnote

1. Both the Hebrew word *chashab* and the Greek word *logizomai* have this sense of bookkeeping, not to mention the immediate context about reckoning wages. *Logizomai* can be translated variously as "compute," "account," "reckon," "impute," "esteem," and "credit."

PENAL SUBSTITUTION

*But he was wounded for our transgressions;
he was crushed for our iniquities; upon him
was the chastisement that brought us peace,
and with his stripes we are healed. All we like
sheep have gone astray; we have turned every
one to his own way; and Yahweh has laid on
him the iniquity of us all. —Isaiah 53:5–6*

Big ideas are usually controversial. Galileo nearly got lynched for saying that the earth went around the sun, and it was two hundred years before he was forgiven. At various times in the last few centuries, you would have found a massive majority disagreeing that the earth was round, that light traveled, that gravity was real, and that electrons existed. With theological concepts, it is even more true: The biggest debates in church history have been over the most important beliefs, like the oneness of God, the divinity and humanity of Jesus, and justification by faith. So it is no great surprise that the notion of "penal substitution"—that Christ took the penalty for our sins when he died on the cross—is so hotly debated today. Important ideas always are.

A common tendency, when faced with a debate between two groups with letters after their names, is to hide under the bed and wait for it to pass. But this is a white flag of surrender; it means that anyone could torpedo the central beliefs of Christianity simply by writing an article questioning them. So those of us who care about the gospel need to engage with issues like this, and "contend for the faith that was once for all delivered to the saints" (Jude 3). Did Jesus suffer a penalty for sin (penal)? Did he die in our place (substitution)? And was God actually responsible for it all? These are huge questions. Fortunately for us, we have Isaiah 53 to help us find out.

In this one explosive chapter, Isaiah answers all three questions. First, he shows us in no uncertain terms that the Messiah would suffer a penalty for sin. Look at the language of verse 5: the Servant was "wounded" for transgressions, "crushed" for iniquities, "chastised" for the sake of peace, and he brought healing through his "stripes" (a term that literally meant the black and blue bruise on the skin where the wound was). Isaiah is not just describing a consequence of sin, but a penalty or a punishment that, somehow, corresponds to transgressions that have been committed and a peace that is needed. So the cross is penal—the Servant suffers a penalty for sin.

But second, it is also substitutionary, because of the tiny little words I missed in the previous paragraph. Look again: wounded for *our* transgressions, crushed for *our* iniquities, the chastisement that brought *us* peace, *we* are healed. The Servant was not punished because he had committed sins, but because we had; it was us, not him, who needed healing and peace with God. If you think about it, Jesus lived a sinless life, so there was no sin in him that needed punishing. So if you realize that the cross is penal, then you pretty much have to believe it is a substitution as well. Isaiah certainly did.

Yet he goes further. Not only does Jesus suffer the penalty for our sin, but the sin was laid on him, and the punishment poured on him, by Yahweh. This is the bit that modern people don't like, but Isaiah could not be clearer:

Yahweh has laid on him the iniquity of us all. (53:6)

Yet it was the will of Yahweh to crush him; he has put him to grief. (53:10)

We might wonder how this process works and even what sort of God could hate sin and love people so much that he was prepared to "crush" Jesus and "put him to grief," but one thing we cannot do is pretend it isn't there. Isaiah insists that Yahweh was one day going to punish the Servant for the sins of the people. In the shadow of Calvary, we can see what Isaiah never could—that this meant punishing not just a faithful servant, but his own Son.

This sounds like a complete tragedy. How could any of this make Jesus "satisfied," as Isaiah puts it, or even bring Yahweh "pleasure"? Well, imagine a city that insists on having a nuclear power reactor against the protests of an environmental campaigner and his son. The people of the city riot and threaten to kill them, calling them every name under the sun for opposing them, and eventually the campaigner and his son leave them to it, moving thousands of miles away. Then there is an accident. Just as the campaigner had predicted, the city faces nuclear meltdown, and thousands of lives are at risk; the only way they can be saved is for someone to enter the nuclear reactor itself and realign the power rods, but such an operation would expose the technician to a lethal dose of radiation poisoning. So no one in the city volunteers.

Then, in an amazing act of grace, the father and son consider the trauma of the city and decide that the son will fly across the country, enter the nuclear reactor himself, sacrifice his life to radiation poisoning, and realign the rods himself. It costs the father his son, and the son his life, to rescue the very people who had rejected them. With the son slowly vomiting and choking to death, you might expect both father and son to regret their choice. But instead, there is a deep joy in both of them, because the sacrifice of one has brought salvation to many. To the astonishment of all those watching the footage, as the son takes his last breath, he is whispering in triumph into his mobile phone. "Father," he says, "it is finished."

> Out of the anguish of his soul he shall see and be satisfied; by his knowledge shall the righteous one, my servant, make many to be accounted righteous, and he shall bear their iniquities. (Isa. 53:11)

REDEMPTION

*In him we have redemption through his
blood, the forgiveness of our trespasses,
according to the riches of his grace, which
he lavished upon us. —Ephesians 1:7–8*

Some words become so religious, you forget what they mean. In the first century, "baptism" meant drenching in liquid, "church" meant the congregation of Israel in any given locality, and "bearing your cross" meant walking to your death carrying the symbol of execution. As the centuries passed, though, these powerful meanings became softened: sprinkling a baby with water, an ornate stone building, or coping with a headache, respectively. When words and phrases lose their original context, they can lose their power as well.

A classic example is "redemption." Ask a random handful of Christians to explain it, and you will probably get some rather vague responses: "salvation," perhaps, or even "justification." Yet those same people, if you asked them to use the word *redeem* in an everyday sentence, would know exactly what it means. They would be familiar with redeeming grocery clubcard points (giving something in exchange for something else) and redeeming mortgages (paying off all remaining debts). They would know that a goalkeeper who had let in a howler could redeem himself (cancel out the effects of previous mistakes) by making a superb save late in the game. They might also talk about people having redeeming features (good things which offset their weaknesses) or about finding redemption (achieving freedom and wholeness after a period of imprisonment or oppression). They might even have seen *The Shawshank Redemption*, in which the main character is set free from appalling and subhuman captivity to a life of liberty and fulfillment. So they would know exactly what redemption was in everyday usage. It's just that it might never have occurred to them that all of these things were achieved for them by Jesus at the cross.

They were. Think about it. God gave Jesus in exchange for you and me, just like we give clubcard points in exchange for groceries. In doing so, God canceled all debts that were outstanding against our account, like we clear our outstanding mortgages. He also canceled out the effects of all our previous mistakes and made Jesus our redeeming feature, the one who offsets and overcomes our weaknesses. Not only that, but he brought us out of imprisonment into a place of wholeness and liberty, thereby rescuing us from sin's power as well as from its punishment. If we just stop and consider what "redemption" means in English, we have a huge mountain range of truth opened up to us.

For the highest peak, however, we need to think like a Jew for a moment. The biblical concept of redemption comes from the exodus: the liberation of two million Hebrew slaves from the oppression of their Egyptian masters. This act of deliverance, orchestrated by God, might be a little fuzzy in our modern minds, but to Paul and his readers the picture would have been exquisitely sharp: God's chosen people, who had been subject to crushing enslavement, abuse, and infanticide for generations, being set free from slavery through the most terrifying display of raw power the world has ever seen. Frequently in the Old Testament, this is the background for the word *redemption*:

> *I will deliver you from slavery to them, and*
> *I will* redeem *you with an outstretched arm*
> *and with great acts of judgment. (Ex. 6:6)*

> *It is because Yahweh loves you and is keeping the*
> *oath that he swore to your fathers, that Yahweh*
> *has brought you out with a mighty hand and*
> redeemed *you from the house of slavery, from*
> *the hand of Pharaoh king of Egypt. (Deut. 7:8)*

The Israelites experienced deliverance, but also redemption; they were brought out, but they were also bought out, ransomed from slavery by almighty God himself.

Interestingly, in passages like these, the emphasis is not on the transaction, but on the state of freedom that results from it. (This is why neither Moses nor Paul make any reference to a ransom being paid "to" anyone—that is simply a misunderstanding of the metaphor.)[1] In fact, both in the exodus and throughout Scripture, the redemption metaphor focuses on what the ransom was *from* and what it was *for*, not on whom or what it was paid *to*. When Paul talks in his letters about redemption, he is making the same point: We, like the Israelites, have been bought by God, set free from our slavery to a hostile power who was intent on destroying us completely, and redeemed from an endless period of imprisonment that had put our freedom and our very humanity at risk. So as we look behind us at the powers that held us captive, crushed beyond recognition and forced to liberate us into glorious freedom, we cannot help but marvel at the cross and at the great Redeemer who died there.

In him we have redemption through his blood, the forgiveness of our trespasses, according to the riches of his grace. Let's not forget it!

Endnote

1. Worrying about this is like the moment when talk-show host Alan Partridge is told that his interviewee felt "like a pawn in the political chess game," and responds by asking, "Who were the bishops?"

COFFEE BREAK:

WAIT AND WORSHIP

Ever since the exodus, the people of God have been singing redemption hymns—songs of joy, celebrating the way Yahweh has ransomed us from slavery and brought us into freedom. To get a sense of God's sweeping acts of rescue, read through Exodus 15:1–18, written by Moses around 1500 BC, and then reflect on the following two hymns, written by the outstanding young songwriter Matt Giles in 2007. We are still worshipping the same redeemer God!

> O redemption! Sweet redemption!
> Satan has no hold on me.
> Now I have indemnity; my
> Debt is paid, and I am free!
> So impoverished and desp'rate,
> In my sins I should have died;
> Yet my King's eternal ransom
> Did my every need provide!
>
> O the cross! My final plea!
> Nought else to offer thee
> But what Christ did for me.
> A million sins incurred my fall,
> But Christ died once, and crushed them all!

(From the hymn "Redemption" © Honeycomb Music 2007)

> Forever I'll proclaim the cross,
> Where Christ retrieved what once was lost.
> To sin and death I was a slave,
> Till he redeemed me from the grave!
> The Lord laid my iniquities
> On him to bring me life and peace.

His blood was shed to set me free;
He purchased me,
And paid the price at Calvary!

It cannot help but humble me
To see his righteous majesty
As humbly he departs his throne
To claim the cross I should have known ...
In heav'n shall I behold the scars
Of hands that orchestrate the stars,
And I will humbly bow the knee
Before his throne
And worship him eternally!

(From the hymn "Forever I'll Proclaim the Cross" © Honeycomb Music 2007)

IN CHRIST

*Blessed be the God and Father of our
Lord Jesus Christ, who has blessed us in
Christ with every spiritual blessing in the
heavenly places. —Ephesians 1:3*

You are currently traveling at sixty thousand miles an hour. That's about the speed of a bullet, and it would get you from London to Edinburgh in twenty-five seconds. In the time it takes you to read this narrative, you will be about five thousand miles from where you were when you started, even if you're just sitting on the sofa. You are flying through the Milky Way's outer spirals like a slingshot, being sucked around the sun by a force you cannot even imagine, and you're also turning round in a circle slowly; even if you were to stay where you are right now, with your eyes fixed on the wall, in six hours' time you would be at right angles to where you are at the moment. Weirder still, you are doing absolutely nothing to cause any of these things. You're probably not even aware of them.

The reason, of course, is that you are in something much bigger than you. It's called Earth, and it is doing all the work. Because you are "in" it, you do everything it does, which means that you are currently traveling vast distances at breakneck speed without even knowing it, in ways that would be totally impossible if you were "out" of it. Amazing, really.

If you think that's amazing, prepare to be re-amazed at being part of Jesus. Because you are in Christ, countless things are true of you that you have done nothing to cause and may not even be aware of. Each of them is only true because you are "in him," and together they form the most glorious list of blessings it is possible to have. That's the world of Ephesians 1.

Because you're in Christ, you are more blessed than you can possibly imagine. It's a simple formula, really: Jesus has been given every spiritual blessing, you are in Jesus, therefore you have been given every spiritual blessing. Flick through some of them with me.

You were chosen in Christ before there was anything else at all: before the wheel, before the moon, God chose you—and not because you were holy and blameless, but because in Christ, God was going to *make* you holy and blameless. You were given a destiny of being adopted through Christ, legally brought into God's family as one of Jesus' little brothers and sisters. You were blessed with glorious grace in Christ, which was inevitable, really, because being in Christ without grace would be like being on Earth without gravity. You were redeemed in Christ, having been bought out of sin by his blood. You had his plan revealed to you in Christ: Jesus not only knew the plan, he *was* the plan, which means we who are in him have front-row seats, as all things are united (you've guessed it) in Christ. You were given an inheritance in Christ, which couldn't really be larger; since Jesus is the heir of the whole world, participating in his inheritance makes the Rockefeller children look small-time. Finally, all this was confirmed in Christ with the Holy Spirit—the deposit that guarantees the transaction, the royal seal that confirms the king's handwriting, the engagement ring that promises the marriage is coming. All in Christ.

The astonishing thing about all of this is that you and I contribute nothing whatever to it. We bring as much to our salvation as we do to the momentum of Earth. We couldn't choose ourselves before the foundation of the world; we weren't even there. Nor could we give ourselves a destiny, redeem ourselves, find out God's plan, or wrangle our way into sharing Jesus' inheritance. We could try, but we would fall flat on our faces. Only in Christ are any of these blessings, let alone all of them, available.

To illustrate, take something that people simply cannot do: flying.[1] For thousands of years, people have seen birds doing it and tried it themselves, but all the attempts, from Daedalus and Icarus onward, tell the same story. Our arm muscles are just not big enough, and there's a trail of corpses to prove it. If I was to try and jump off Beachy Head tomorrow and fly to France, it wouldn't matter how hard I tried, or how strenuously I had trained, I would plunge to my death just as quickly as the person who made no effort whatsoever. That's you and me outside of Christ. Complete no-hopers, and dead to boot.

Now imagine I go to Gatwick and get on a Boeing 747. As I buy my ticket, I am making the admission that my own strength cannot get me to Paris, and I need to get inside something that can. So, in faith that the plane can carry me, I get on board and immediately notice something astonishing. None of the passengers on the plane are flapping their arms. Quite the opposite: They are all sitting down, reading the paper and drinking orange juice. It is almost as if they are completely secure in their *position* and believe that they will get to Paris and receive all the blessings of France, entirely on the basis of what they are in, rather than what they do. Which, of course, they will.

Our entire salvation is in Jesus. We have been chosen and predestined and adopted and redeemed and sealed in him. So our confidence in God's love and our hope of sharing in the new creation are not based in our disciplines, our families, or our churches, as important as those things are. They are in Christ.

Endnote

1. I am grateful to John Groves for this illustration.

THE AVALANCHE OF GRACE

*For by grace you have been saved through
faith. And this is not your own doing; it is
the gift of God, not a result of works, so that
no one may boast. —Ephesians 2:8–9*

The grace of God is an unstoppable avalanche that sweeps all in its path. It changes the landscape so dramatically that it is hard to remember what things looked like before. In Ephesians 2 alone, God's grace is responsible for raising dead people to life, seating them with Christ in heavenly places, giving them good works to do, and uniting people who wouldn't have touched each other with a ten-foot pole. In twenty-two verses, the avalanche of grace changes a morgue into a temple. Watch.

The chapter starts abruptly: "And you were dead." Without passages like this, we would probably describe our rescue as gradually waking up to God and reaching out for his help, like a man at sea realizing he needs help and gratefully accepting a lifeline. But Ephesians says we were far worse than that. We were dead (2:1), following Satan (2:2), and "children of wrath" (2:3). We were not drowning in our sin, we had already drowned. So the picture of God's grace is not of a coast guard throwing us a lifeline which we might or might not grab onto, but of someone walking through a graveyard raising corpses to life. God, "even when we were dead in our trespasses, made us alive together with Christ" (2:5).

By itself, that is quite an impressive avalanche of grace. You and I would be quite chuffed with raising people from the dead. To God, however, that is just the beginning. He doesn't leave us former corpses to our own devices but incorporates us into Christ (as we saw in the previous narrative) and seats us with Christ in heavenly places. Why? "So that in the coming ages he might show the immeasurable riches of his grace" (2:7). God showing us his grace is not just the basis for our salvation, it's the reason for it.

Now, it might sound a bit strange that we are "seated in heavenly places," since our bodies are still on earth. But consider a check-in queue at an airport. Last summer, Rachel and I were in an airport queue where we had economy tickets. Suddenly, a steward appeared and told us that we had been seated in Business Class because of our friend Rebecca, who is a pilot. In a purely literal sense, we were still exactly where we had been before, surrounded by the same people and in the same queue. But the reality was that our destiny had changed, and that meant everything was different: We started talking excitedly about it, and instead of dreading the flight as seven hours of boredom, we began really looking forward to it. When you and I are seated with Christ in heavenly places, our bodies remain where they are, at least for the moment, but everything else—our destiny, our desires, our behavior—is transformed completely. Because of grace.

In the meantime, there are things for us to do. God's grace shouldn't lead to inactivity; if it does, then we've misunderstood something. It is there to be shared with everyone, so that the grace of God might be seen as glorious in every country, school, hospital, and office, whether in preaching or healing or integrity or kindness. The avalanche is not just for the sake of it.

One of the most powerful things that the avalanche of grace does is to unite Gentiles with Jews in the church. In the Jerusalem temple, there was a stone partition between Jewish and Gentile areas and a notice that said any Gentiles passing that point would be responsible for their own deaths.[1] Hardly a ringing welcome. Yet here was Paul, proclaiming that because of the grace of God in Christ, Gentiles were able to join Israel, to share in God's promises, and to be part of his temple (redefined as his people), without any enmity, rivalry, or partition. This was what the avalanche of grace was for: "that he might create in himself one new man in place of the two … thereby killing the hostility" (2:15–16).

The bringing together of Jew and Gentile in the church to be "one new man" is stunning. It leaves no room for racism in the people of God, or for that matter sexism, ageism, or any other type of separation. Instead, the grace and wisdom of God are shown by his creation of a community where there are old and young, black and white, male and female, Jew and Gentile, cleaner and politician, all worshipping the God of grace together (as Paul will explain further in Ephesians 3).[2]

In the end, you see, God's avalanche of grace is unstoppable. Life beats death; grace trumps race; oneness defeats division; and the work of Christ turns a graveyard into a graceyard, a mortuary into a sanctuary. This is not our own doing—it is by grace, so that no one may boast. For by grace we have been saved through faith.

Endnotes

1. John Stott, *The Message of Ephesians*, (Leicester, UK: IVP, 1991), 92.

2. It is hard to overstate Paul's campaign against racism in the early church. Besides Ephesians, Galatians and Romans were deeply concerned with it, and "there is neither Jew nor Greek" became something of a motto for him (see Gal. 3:28; Col. 3:11). His home church, Antioch, was also a model of "one new man" leadership, combining black and white, Jews, Greeks, and Romans (Acts 13:1–2).

OUR GREAT HIGH PRIEST

*He holds his priesthood permanently, because
he continues forever. Consequently, he is able to
save to the uttermost those who draw near to
God through him, since he always lives to make
intercession for them. —Hebrews 7:24-25*

The way God set things up in Israel, you couldn't be a priest and a king at the same time. It was impossible. Priests had to be purely from the tribe of Levi, and kings had to be purely from the tribe of Judah, so you couldn't be both.

With two exceptions. The first one, Melchizedek, was a mysterious figure who appears before the tribal system, and whose entire purpose seems to have been to point forward to the second one. The second one was Jesus, who was a king from the tribe of Judah (because of his birth), yet became a priest in the order of Melchizedek by the power of an indestructible life (because of his death and resurrection). Jesus combined the two key roles in a totally unexpected and seemingly impossible way: priest and king at the same time. Confused? So were the Hebrews.

We might wonder whether it matters, but it matters enormously. Jesus needed to be a king, because if he wasn't, he couldn't be the Messiah, couldn't be given authority over the earth, couldn't rule the nations and crush God's enemies. But he also needed to be a priest, because if he wasn't, he couldn't present sacrifices to God on behalf of the people, and he certainly couldn't make them holy. If he wasn't a king, he couldn't be our Lord. But if he wasn't a priest, he couldn't be our Savior.

This explains why the writer to the Hebrews makes such a big deal out of him being both. The priests of Levi, like Aaron, had to be replaced each generation because they died. Jesus, the one who had the power of an indestructible life, stands to the Levitical priesthood like Mount Everest stands to a sand castle—while one is temporary and needs continual replacement, Jesus towers over it and "holds his priesthood permanently, because he continues forever." And as a result, he is able to "save to the uttermost" in a way that the priests of Levi never could.

So what did priests do? Well, there were at least four aspects to their work, and Jesus trumps them all. The most well-known thing they did was to sacrifice. It was the priests, and no one else, who were allowed to approach the Tent of Meeting, pass through the curtain, and make atonement for the people. We tend to remember the blood of the animal, but in the tabernacle there were two things needed for a sacrifice of atonement: an animal and a priest. Now, here's the bombshell that Hebrews announces: *Jesus was both*. He was the innocent sacrifice, but he was also the high priest who offered it. And because he was sinless, his sacrifice was able to cleanse what the Levitical sacrifices never could: not just our sins, but our consciences as well (Heb. 9:13–14).

The next thing priests did was representing people to God and God to people. There's a powerful story about this in Numbers 16, when the judgment of God falls on Israel, and Aaron has to act quickly to save them:

So Aaron ... ran into the midst of the assembly.
And behold, the plague had already begun
among the people. And he put on the incense
and made atonement for the people. And he
stood between the dead and the living, and
the plague was stopped. (Num. 16:47–48)

Priests, being human, could fully represent people to God. But Jesus, being fully God and fully human, can represent perfectly both ways. He can sympathize with our weaknesses, yet without condoning our sins. He is the perfect go-between. (That, incidentally, is why we don't pray to God through saints or through Mary. Jesus is the only mediator we need.) He can stand between the dead and the living and save us from God's judgment.

Third, priests blessed the people. In Leviticus 9, right after the first sacrifices are presented according to the old covenant, Aaron lifts up his hand and blesses the people, showing that the offering has been accepted. Immediately, the glory of Yahweh appears, and fire comes out from his presence. So it is interesting that right after making the first (and only) sacrifice of the new covenant, Jesus ...

... led them out as far as Bethany, and lifting up
his hands he blessed them. (Luke 24:50)

Within a few days, the glory of Yahweh had appeared, and the fire of his presence had come to his people (Acts 2:3). Make of that what you will.

Finally, priests prayed for the people. They had to; the people were sinful, and their salvation depended on it. That's why there was incense in the tabernacle and why it had to be kept burning 24-7. But the priests couldn't pray the whole time. They were human, and they had plenty of other things to do. Jesus, however, faces no such time pressures. So, as we saw at the beginning of this narrative, he is able to save completely everyone who comes to God through him, because he is always interceding for them. Wherever we are right now, and whatever we're doing in the next twenty-four hours, we have an advocate, our Great High Priest at the right hand of God, who is continually praying for us. Hallelujah!

COFFEE BREAK:

I'm not aware of any song that expresses the high priestly work of Jesus better than "Before the Throne of God Above," written by Charitie L. Bancroft in 1863. The second half of verse two is one of the most outstanding sections of any hymn.

Before the throne of God above
I have a strong and perfect plea:
A great high Priest whose Name is Love
Who ever lives and pleads for me.
My name is graven on His hands,
My name is written on His heart.
I know that while in Heaven He stands
No tongue can bid me thence depart.

When Satan tempts me to despair
And tells me of the guilt within,
Upward I look and see Him there
Who made an end of all my sin.
Because the sinless Savior died
My sinful soul is counted free.
For God the just is satisfied
To look on Him and pardon me.

Behold Him there the risen Lamb,
My perfect spotless righteousness,
The great unchangeable I AM,
The King of glory and of grace,
One in Himself I cannot die.
My soul is purchased by His blood,
My life is hid with Christ on high,
With Christ my Savior and my God!

ACT FIVE
RESTORATION AND HOPE

REPENTANCE AND BAPTISM

*Now when they heard this they were cut to
the heart, and said to Peter and the rest of the
apostles, "Brothers, what shall we do?" And Peter
said to them, "Repent and be baptized every
one of you in the name of Jesus Christ for the
forgiveness of your sins, and you will receive
the gift of the Holy Spirit." —Acts 2:37–38*

So what next? The practically minded among us will probably be asking that question by now: I have reflected on lots of GodStories, and I understand the gospel, but what am I actually supposed to *do*? Well, if that's your question, you're in good company. That's what the crowd wanted to know on the day of Pentecost, and it's exactly the right thing to ask. And thanks to Peter, we have a very clear answer. Repent and be baptized, every one of you, for the forgiveness of your sins, and you will receive the gift of the Holy Spirit.

Simple, really. Two things: Turn your life around to follow God, and get drenched in water. Somehow, over the generations, that very straightforward response became more complicated: get circumcised, obey Jewish food laws, do penance, say certain prayers, read your Bible, believe certain doctrines, cut your hair, stop drinking. But none of those things were in the mix originally. According to Peter on the day of Pentecost, and to Jesus and Paul and the rest of the apostles, the right response to the gospel was simply repentance and baptism. That's it.

Repentance means turning around. I am writing this narrative in an English town called Shrewsbury. The town is full of stunning Tudor buildings and a thoroughly incomprehensible one-way traffic system which has completely baffled me. About an hour ago, this resulted in me driving directly toward a white van, who fortunately saw me in time and allowed me the time and space to *repent*, to do a complete U-turn and get myself going in the correct direction. I followed the system round the town for five minutes, and then (to my horror) did it again in a different place. This time, the bus driver staring at me was somewhat less sympathetic, and I was forced once again into total *repentance*, this time with rather more people watching.

Here's the point: Repenting involves both a change of mind and a change of direction. Obviously I needed to change my mind about which direction to head in, because if I didn't, I would never have changed where the car was pointing. But equally, if I had trundled round the corner toward that bus driver a few minutes ago, thinking that I was going the wrong way round the system but not doing anything about it, it would have resulted in a hefty insurance claim. If I had driven straight toward him while saying the words "I'm sorry," that wouldn't have done much good either. Repentance for me in my car, and for us in our lives, means actually doing a complete U-turn and heading in the opposite direction. It means driving toward God rather than driving toward ourselves. It means agreeing that, in our time management and conversations and finances and sex lives, Jesus is Lord and we are not.

So repentance is ultimately something that takes place in the heart and in the mind, but which always results in transformed behavior. The other half of the response, however, is clearly and deliberately physical: baptism in water. However much some people might object to it, claiming that it sounds too traditional or magical or ceremonial, baptism is the one other thing that all believers in the New Testament do in response to the gospel. In fact, taken at face value, Scripture suggests that baptism is part of how we become a Christian, rather than merely an outward demonstration that we already have. Look:

> We were buried therefore with him by baptism
> *into death, in order that, just as Christ was raised*
> *from the dead by the glory of the Father, we*
> *too might walk in newness of life. (Rom. 6:4)*

> *Having been buried with him in* baptism, in
> which you were also raised with him *through*
> *faith in the powerful working of God, who*
> raised him from the dead. (Col. 2:12)

> Baptism, *which corresponds to this*, now saves
> you, *not as a removal of dirt from the body but as*
> *an appeal to God for a good conscience, through*
> *the resurrection of Jesus Christ. (1 Peter 3:21)*

Now, I know some Christian traditions don't think like this, either because they baptize people before they come to saving faith (as infants) or because they think of baptism as "just a symbol." But there the texts are, staring us in the face. Baptism is more than a symbol, because it actually *does* something. And although we know that the brigand on the cross was saved without being baptized, we also know that he was the only one in the whole New Testament for whom that was true—and that he had a pretty compelling excuse!

So how does it work? Do we have to get baptized in order to become a disciple or not? To answer that, let's take a similar-sounding question: Do you have to digest your food in order to have eaten it? Now, I guess that question sounds idiotic to us because we don't know anyone who has ever eaten their food and *not* digested it (except perhaps, as with the brigand on the cross, people who were dying in the process). So how would we answer? Think about it for a moment, and then apply your answers to baptism and becoming a disciple.

We would presumably say (1) that digesting food is not the same as eating it, but (2) it is still part of eating it. We probably (3) couldn't imagine why anyone wouldn't digest their food, since that was where things were headed as soon as they swallowed it. We might admit (4) that it was theoretically possible to eat and not digest, but without being able to imagine how this was possible unless they had died in the process—and we might say (5) that if anyone said they had not digested a certain meal, we would assume they hadn't eaten it properly either. Finally, we might note (6) that digesting always followed chewing and swallowing, so if someone said they had digested their food before they had eaten it, that would display a misunderstanding of what both "digesting" and "eating" actually were.

According to Jesus and the apostles, the same things are true of baptism. It is (1) not the same as becoming a disciple, but (2) it is part of it, and (3) it is very weird to think of anyone repenting and not getting baptized as a believer, because that was where the repentance was heading. We might concede (4) that it was possible in theory to repent and not get baptized, but it is hard to fathom why or how unless the person was dying at the time. Similarly, (5) if someone refuses to get baptized, it suggests that their repentance might not be complete in the first place, and (6) baptism cannot come before repentance, since it is always a response to it.[1] So although baptism alone doesn't make someone a disciple, if it has never happened then it means something odd has happened somewhere, and it needs to be sorted out.

Of course, it is impossible in such a small space to be thorough in addressing such a controversial subject. But if you read through the relevant verses in the New Testament, I think you will find that it doesn't sound like it was very controversial among the apostles. If someone had asked Jesus or Paul or James what they needed to do to respond to the gospel of God, they would all have given a very similar answer. And Peter would have been crystal clear: Just repent and be baptized, every one of you, and your sins will be forgiven, and the Holy Spirit will live inside you. It's that simple.

Endnote

1. I am aware that some Christians do not see it this way, seeing baptism as a covenant sign like circumcision. Nonetheless, baptism is clearly presented in Scripture as a response to faith, and there are no New Testament examples of people being "baptized" without first hearing and responding to the gospel; the same is clearly not true of circumcision. For a watertight case (no pun intended), see Wayne Grudem, *Systematic Theology* (Leicester, UK: IVP, 1994), 966–87.

THE BATTLE FOR BEAUTY

And the twelve gates were twelve pearls, each of the gates made of a single pearl, and the street of the city was pure gold, transparent as glass. —Revelation 21:21

You can usually tell a lot about someone by their reaction to beauty. God, who is perfect in every way, is deeply excited about it and has committed himself to creating it, delighting in it, and restoring it. Animals are indifferent to it; even the most intelligent monkeys don't gaze in wonder at paintings or waterfalls, and there are no postimpressionist chipmunks or puffin poetry anthologies. Satan absolutely hates it. You might never have noticed this, but one of the most visible results of his deceitful stunt in Eden was that the most stunning garden in history became off-limits.

Among people, the appreciation of beauty can act as an indicator of maturity. Babies see paint and food as things to be played with, but by school age, children can already use their creativity to experiment with them, and in adulthood, some people spend small fortunes on gourmet meals and Renaissance art. Infants are so transfixed by novelty that they don't really register a gorgeous sunrise, but by our teens, this has reversed, so that we are able to stare at the same night sky that has been there for thousands of years and remain open-mouthed at its splendor. However, no matter how mature or godly we are, our delight in beauty is always coupled with a sense of longing, whether we are admiring art or creation itself. It is hard to describe, but I'm sure you know what I mean: a twinge in our spirits, even an ache, that the whole world ought to be like this all the time, but it isn't. We bear the image of our creator God, and that means we have a passionate desire for beauty, both to create it and to appreciate it. So when we look out upon a world so often marred by ugliness, our souls tell us it shouldn't be like that.

Our souls are right. You see, the whole of creation is the battleground in an enormous fight for beauty that has been going on since the very beginning. We humans, fickle creatures that we are, have fought on both sides in this battle, which is why we feel so confused about it sometimes. Adam and Eve were the original gamekeepers-turned-poachers, quite literally, and we have continued their ambiguous relationship with beauty ever since: painting yet polluting, dancing yet deforesting, composing yet combusting. Even contemporary art, which is often deliberately shocking and unaesthetic so as to challenge the idea of beauty itself, demonstrates the tension. We were made for a world of sheer beauty, but the world we live in now is a battleground for it.

It has not always been like this. When first created, the earth is formless and void and dark, but as soon as Yahweh starts speaking, beauty spills out all over the place, and it is beauty that still transfixes us today—light, clouds, sea, trees, stars, fish, birds, animals. You rarely meet an artist who is completely happy with their work, but of God it is said repeatedly, "He saw that it was good." In the next scene, Genesis 2, the camera pans in a little closer so you can see the aesthetic dimension of creation more clearly, and the writer starts to inform us of otherwise pointless details like the beautiful stones found near each of the rivers (2:11–12) and the fact that the trees were "pleasant to the sight" (2:9) and even that "the gold of that land is good" (2:12). To be honest, as the garden is described, it is the attractiveness of God's creation, rather than its moral purity or anything else, that captures our attention. In six days, God has unstoppably turned formlessness into ravishing beauty.

Things all change after the assault in Genesis 3. The garden is barred, creation is cursed, and the most beautiful created thing there is, the one that bears God's image, is corrupted. Beauty is still there, of course, after the fall—the following chapters tell us of people learning to play pipes and guitars and develop architecture—but it is shrouded, as if someone had thrown a dust sheet over Michelangelo's *David*. So Yahweh gets to work in the battle for beauty and begins restoring the twin wonders of creation and creativity.

Most of this battle centers on the land of Israel and the temple in Jerusalem in particular. Israel, as we know, is a land flowing with milk and honey, a land where clusters of grapes are so large they require a pole to carry them. But before Israel even gets to the land, Yahweh prepares them for their mission to demonstrate God's beauty to the world by commissioning a tabernacle of intricate design and sumptuous embroidery. Have you ever got stuck in the back half of Exodus and wondered why the acacia wood and fine twisted linen, the purple and the scarlet, the skillful weaving and the jewelled garments "for glory and for beauty" (Ex. 28:2) are worth describing in such detail? It is because the tabernacle was intended to display the splendor of Yahweh. This is even truer when it comes to the temple, which became the centerpiece of God's battle for beauty, built of endless cedar and gold and festooned with golden pomegranates. I doubt if anywhere in history has been such a carnival of the arts: elaborate architecture, decorated with expensive metalwork, woodwork, and cloth, before which all manner of poems were written, songs sung, and dances performed, with musical instruments in abundance and the fragrance of incense throughout. Because of the beauty of Yahweh, the temple where he lived was unimaginably exquisite.

Yet it was not ultimate. For in the prophetic and apocalyptic writings, particularly those that describe a new heaven and a new earth, an even greater level of beauty is described, as the glory of God begins to fill the whole earth and not just the temple. It will even affect the animal kingdom, as lions will lie with lambs and eat straw like oxen (Isa. 11:6–7). It will be the moment when the dust sheet comes back off the *David* and the audience gasps as the sculpture is now in full color, bright and radiant, far outstripping the original. According to Revelation 21, it will be like a bride, perfectly adorned for her husband, gleaming like jasper, clear as crystal. This magnificent city will be perfectly cubic to please the eye, with gates of pearl, streets of glasslike gold, and foundations of a dazzling array of precious stones, filled with a light so bright it replaces the sun. None of this is functional; it is simply there to be beautiful. Like art. And, to an extent, like God.

For now, we still live on the battlefield. But ultimately, imagination and creativity, both God's ideas, will triumph; and ugliness, one of Satan's chief weapons, will be banished forever. And God will win, once and for all, the battle for beauty.

SANCTIFICATION

*But thanks be to God, that you who were once
slaves of sin ... having been set free from sin,
have become slaves of righteousness. I am
speaking in human terms, because of your
natural limitations. For just as you once presented
your members as slaves to impurity and to
lawlessness leading to more lawlessness, so now
present your members as slaves to righteousness
leading to sanctification. —Romans 6:17–19*

Be who you are. That's the New Testament approach to sanctification (or growing in holiness). It doesn't matter who you ask, increasing in godliness is simply a question of knowing who you are and then living that way. Peter says we've been called out of darkness into light, so we should abstain from the passions of the flesh. John says we're children of God, so we should live like him. Hebrews says we've been sanctified once for all, so we should pursue holiness. But the biggest champion of the idea is Paul: You've become slaves to righteousness, so act like it. That's how sanctification happens.

His argument here in Romans 6 is tremendously important, and it comes in three simple, profound steps, the first of which is that you have been set free from sin. You see, even though it is true that Christians have been released from sin, Satan does his best to convince them they're not, and lots of them believe him: Fearful people believe they'll always be fearful, porn addicts that they'll never overcome lust, the abused that they'll never be able to forgive. So even though those people have been set free from sin in Christ, they don't know it, so they never live that way.[1]

I saw a powerful picture of this in Devon a few years ago. I was driving down a lane with my cousin Seb when a young boy walked past holding a rope, attached to which was a bull the size of a garden shed. He was massive. He dwarfed our car and was certainly many times too large for anyone to control with a piece of rope through its nose, so I was quite worried. Yet the bull seemed blissfully unaware of his power and meekly followed the boy, which I thought was very odd. I later learned, however, that farmers sometimes train bulls by attaching rope through their noses when they are very young and tying the rope around wooden posts, so that the young bull gets used to the idea that he cannot escape. By the time he is fully grown, he has had so much experience of being enslaved by the rope that he doesn't even know he can break free, which means that these giants can be led by small children without it ever occurring to them to escape. Tragically, many Christians live like that. They have so much experience of being enslaved by sin that they don't even know that, in Christ, they can break free. So children of God can be bound by Satan for years without it ever occurring to them to escape.

Paul is emphatic: You have been set free from sin. That's step one. If you don't know that, then you won't grow in holiness, because you won't realize it's possible. (I speak from experience here. As a teenager, I just didn't believe I could win the battle against lust, until after years of struggling, someone convinced me that it was actually possible to overcome it. Freedom started from that day onward.) But step two is the other side of the coin, and it's just as important. You have not just been released from slavery to sin, you have become a slave to righteousness. Your allegiance has not been removed, it has been transferred.

Let's say you are a British prisoner of war in Germany in 1944. You have spent five years under German command and have spent your days repairing their machinery, building them bridges, obeying their officers, and saluting their flag. Then one day you are liberated by the Allies. Suddenly, your ownership changes, and you become a "slave" to someone else. It would obviously be inappropriate for you to repair German guns and salute German officers now (although through force of habit you would probably do it sometimes without thinking). But it would also be completely inappropriate for you to say that, because you had been set free, you weren't going to work for the Allies either; if you thought like that, it would show that you didn't really understand your liberation, or the war, or both. No, you would immediately set about repairing Allied guns and bridges and obeying Allied officers. Having been set free from serving the Germans, you would immediately start serving the Allies.

We have not only been set free from sin, we have become slaves to righteousness. We may occasionally serve our old master without thinking about it. But when that happens, we remind ourselves of the truth that we have been liberated, and we get on with serving the new master. There's no such thing as neutral, no Switzerland in the spiritual landscape that we can sit in and watch the war. We all fight for something. And in the case of Christians, that something is righteousness.

Step three, then, is simply the application of these two truths: "Present your members as slaves to righteousness leading to sanctification." We're free from sin, we're slaves of righteousness, so we live that way. That's how we pursue holiness. We recognize who we are, we realize what has happened, and we live accordingly. On January 1, 1863, slavery in the Confederate states was officially abolished. Around four million people who had lived their entire lives under the rule of a slavemaster were legally declared "forever free." On January 2, how many slaves were there in the Confederate states? Zero. But how many continued to live as slaves to a master they were no longer legally bound to, because they didn't know they were free? Millions. You can be free from sin and a slave to righteousness, but unless you know it and live like it then your freedom is pretty theoretical.

Sanctification, then, is simple. You've been set free from sin by the blood of Jesus; you've been made a slave to righteousness by the power of God; so present yourselves as the slaves to righteousness you are. Leave your slavemaster, start fighting for the Allies, go on the charge down the Devon lanes. No longer will your actions lead to lawlessness. They'll lead to sanctification.

Endnote

1. For a far more thorough, and extremely biblical, explanation of this whole theme, see the various works of Neil T. Anderson, including *Victory over the Darkness* (Ventura, CA: Regal, 2000) and *The Bondage Breaker* (Eugene, OR: Harvest House, 2000).

OUR CITIZENSHIP IS IN HEAVEN

But our citizenship is in heaven, and from it we await a Savior, the Lord Jesus Christ, who will transform our lowly body to be like his glorious body, by the power that enables him even to subject all things to himself. —Philippians 3:20-21

I don't know whether you've ever had crossed wires with someone, where you say one thing and they misunderstand a word and think you're saying something else. It can be hilarious at times, but it can also be very awkward. If you don't believe me, just watch a conversation between an American and an English person about wearing pants.

"Our citizenship is in heaven" is another example. To some people, this phrase means that, since Christians are ultimately bound for a world in the sky called "heaven," there's no point bothering about the world we live in now. Others react to this by saying that the idea of "heaven" and of us being "citizens" of it are silly, ancient ideas that you would only believe in if you lived before the invention of the dishwasher, so instead, we should focus on making this world better and leave heaven out of it. If the first group, as it is sometimes unkindly said, are at risk of preaching a gospel so heavenly minded it's of no earthly use, the second is in danger of preaching one so earthly minded it's of no heavenly use. The fact is, both groups have completely misunderstood both "heaven" (which is the dwelling place of God, not the final destination of people) and "citizenship."

The Philippians would have known exactly what citizenship was all about. Philippi was a Roman colony in modern-day Greece, an outpost of the empire that was intended to bring Roman rule to the area. Many of the church would have been Roman citizens, some of them soldiers, and they would have been used to living as foreigners in the community, with the purpose of spreading Roman influence. If one of them were to say, "Our citizenship is in Rome," it would not mean that they were otherworldly dreamers who were in Philippi for a few months and couldn't wait to get home. Nor would it mean that they had stopped believing in Rome altogether and had decided to get on with Greek life without it. It would mean that they were Roman through and through, outsiders in a strange land, but *with the purpose of making the strange land more like home* while they waited for the emperor to come.

Which is exactly what Paul means. The church is an outpost of God's empire: a community of people whose passport is stamped "heaven" but who continue to live in a foreign land—earth—with the aim of making that foreign land more like home. We take heaven seriously and live with different aims and different values from the people around us. We also take our citizenship seriously, so instead of hiding under the bed and waiting for rescue (or the rapture?), we live in the world with the intention of changing it. We are there to take the empire, or the kingdom of God, everywhere we go while we wait for the Emperor to come.

Notice, also, the small word *our*. You and I share our citizenship in heaven with lots of other people who have the same passports we do, and that's an important part of this GodStory. Living in a foreign country is exhausting, and sometimes discouraging, so God designed the local church: little outposts of heaven, scattered throughout the world, where people who share the same passports can regroup, speak their home language, and encourage and equip one another as missionaries to the world around them. Mission is hard, and these outposts are vital for the citizens of heaven. So from the earliest days of the church, Christians (and particularly Paul, who wrote Philippians) planted local churches. For citizens of heaven, they are the most empowering and refreshing places on earth.

Let me illustrate. As a citizen of the UK, I spent a week in Nigeria last year on a human-rights visit, in the course of which I encountered lots of things that made me feel like a foreigner: forty-degree heat, monsoon rain, Islamic Sharia law, eating endless plantains, and the experience of being the only white face in the street. It was exhausting struggling with the heat, the diet, the medicine, and so on. When the trip finished, however, I had the tremendous joy of getting on board the British Airways plane to fly home. I was ushered into this comfortable reclining seat and offered a wide range of very English comforts: tea, a cooked breakfast, a copy of the *Times*. Then a voice came over the speaker, that deep gravelly voice that only British Airways pilots can do: "Good morning. My name is Nigel, and I'll be your captain this morning. We're just in a queue at the moment, but shortly we'll be tootling across the runway and preparing for takeoff. Thank you." There we were, on a runway in the blazing African sun, slap bang in the middle of Nigeria. Yet you couldn't have imagined a more English moment, and I felt like I had already arrived home.

It reinforced my citizenship, recharged my batteries, and refreshed my soul.

The local church is like that—a totally heavenly place in the midst of a very earthly world, a place that reinforces our citizenship and renews our heavenly passports. But here's the thing: If you're not a missionary, it is all a bit pointless. If you're keeping your citizenship quiet, opting out of the struggle to bring heaven to earth in your office or school or family, then coming together with other citizens can seem a waste of time. If I hadn't been in Nigeria for a week, sitting in an aircraft cabin wouldn't have been my idea of fun. But when we're out in the world every day, bringing the empire of God into our cities, then local churches like Philippi—churches which are army barracks, not social clubs—are just what we need. So as citizens, let's bring heaven to earth as we wait for the Emperor to come back:

> *Let your kingdom come near! Let your purpose come about, over the earth in the same way as in heaven! (Matt. 6:10, author's translation)*

CREATION SET FREE

For the creation waits with eager longing for the revealing of the sons of God. For the creation was subjected to futility, not willingly, but because of him who subjected it, in hope that the creation itself will be set free from its bondage to corruption and obtain the freedom of the glory of the children of God. —Romans 8:19–21

I'd like you to think for a moment about the most spectacular place you have ever seen. It could be somewhere you've actually visited, or it could be somewhere in a holiday brochure. My personal choice is the New Zealand South Island, where the mountains are so crisp and the valleys so sweeping you wish *The Lord of the Rings* had excised the hobbits and filmed the scenery for nine hours instead. Yet all of the spectacular sights you pictured, and many more besides—shooting stars, Alpine glaciers, African dawns, thunderstorms—have one thing in common. They are all subjected to futility.

It was Adam's fault. He governed creation poorly, and as a result Yahweh cursed the ground, saying it would produce thorns and thistles. The abundance and fruitfulness that was originally created in the garden was lost and replaced by a world with weeds and stinging nettles and mosquitoes and famine. The curse on creation, just like the curses on man and woman, was God's righteous and inevitable response to the fall.

However, just like the curses on man and woman, the curse on creation was intended to be temporary. Not because God would eventually forget his curse (the serpent, in fact, will remain under it forever), but because he would eventually overcome it. This is the point of the well-known announcement that in the new creation, "no longer will there be anything accursed" (Rev. 22:3). It is also the point that Paul made in the verses we just read: Creation was subjected to futility and decay, but with the wonderful hope that it would one day "obtain the freedom of the glory of the children of God." So creation is under a curse, but only for now. The incorruptible life of Jesus is breaking out everywhere, so much so that eventually the earth itself will be released from its fruitlessness and set free to become what it was originally designed to be.

Now, I don't know about you, but to me this opens up some staggering possibilities. When I consider the Amazon jungle, where every acre has around three hundred species of trees plus three hundred types of other plants, I am given to wonder: If this is what the earth is like when in bondage to decay, what will it look like when it is brought into freedom? If the Grand Tetons and the Serengeti Plain and the California redwoods and the Maldives are subjected to futility for the moment, then what on earth can we expect when Jesus returns to make all things new? Planet Earth, no doubt, will be liberated into levels of wonder and glory that are currently only hinted at. There may also, on top of this, be an outbreak of life and fruitfulness in the rest of the universe, to be explored by a people with infinite amounts of time and no physical constraints on movement. After all, both Old and New Testaments speak of the "heavens," as well as the earth, being renewed (in the plural, this word usually refers to the skies and outer space), and that could well involve the springing to life of planets in galaxies that no man would otherwise ever see. Even if not, though, the glory of the renewed creation will dramatically outstrip that of the present.

This correspondence between failure and futility, or between righteousness and restoration, runs throughout Scripture. The first sin resulted in fruitlessness, and the combined sins of humanity in Noah's day led to much of creation being destroyed. On the other hand, Yahweh's promise of a land flowing with milk and honey was a sign of his favor to his people, and he instructed them that there was a clear correlation between their obedience and their harvests, and even the weather (Lev. 26:3–4). Ever since, the faithfulness of people and the fruitfulness of earth have corresponded to one another. The prophets were so excited about the restoration of God's people and about the effect this would have on creation that they couldn't contain themselves, using quite bizarre images to convey the latter: mountains overflowing with wine (Amos 9:11–15), hills singing and trees clapping their hands (Isa. 55:12–13), and so on. So Paul's announcement that the restoration of humanity would lead to the restoration of creation itself should not come as a surprise. The whole of history has been pointing to it.

Ultimately, although this glorious hope is a motivation for obedience, and although we can dream and speculate how it will be, it is impossible to fathom what creation set free will look like. We have hints in the Bible, but that is all, and that is probably because, when all is said and done, we are trying to imagine the unimaginable. C. S. Lewis put it like this:

> You may have been in a room in which there was a window that looked out on a lovely bay of the sea or a green valley that wound away among the mountains. And in the wall of that room opposite to the window there may have been a looking glass.... And the sea in the mirror, or the valley in the mirror, were in one sense just the same as the real ones: yet at the same time they were somehow different—deeper, more wonderful, more like places in a story: in a story you have never heard but very much want to know. The difference between the old Narnia and the new Narnia was like that. The new one was a deeper country: every rock and flower and blade of grass looked like it meant more. I can't describe it any better than that: if you ever get there you will know what I mean. It was the unicorn who summed up what everyone was feeling. He stamped his right fore-hoof on the ground and neighed, and then cried: "I have come home at last! This is my real country! I belong here. This is the land I have been looking for all my life, though I never knew it till now. The reason why we loved the old Narnia is that it sometimes looked a little like this."[1]

No wonder creation waits "in eager longing." Do you?

Endnote
1. C. S. Lewis, *The Last Battle* (New York: Macmillan, 1970), 171.

COFFEE BREAK:

Most Christians need to think more about eternity. I know I do. It is so easy, when faced with the immediate, to forget the ultimate.

One thing that helps is to meditate on those passages of Scripture that speak about the new heavens and the new earth, so here are a few key ones to get you started. If it helps you, try reading them while listening to the song "There Is a Day" by Nathan Fellingham—it will remind you of the world as it will be.

> *Then the angel showed me the river of the water of life, bright as crystal, flowing from the throne of God and of the Lamb through the middle of the street of the city; also, on either side of the river, the tree of life with its twelve kinds of fruit, yielding its fruit each month. The leaves of the tree were for the healing of the nations. No longer will there be anything accursed, but the throne of God and of the Lamb will be in it, and his servants will worship him. They will see his face, and his name will be on their foreheads. And night will be no more. They will need no light of lamp or sun, for the Lord God will be their light, and they will reign forever and ever. (Rev. 22:1–5)*

> *For I consider that the sufferings of this present time are not worth comparing with the glory that is to be revealed to us. For the creation waits with eager longing for the revealing of the sons of God. For the creation was subjected to futility, not willingly, but because of him who subjected it, in hope that the*

creation itself will be set free from its bondage to corruption and obtain the freedom of the glory of the children of God. For we know that the whole creation has been groaning together in the pains of childbirth until now. And not only the creation, but we ourselves, who have the firstfruits of the Spirit, groan inwardly as we wait eagerly for adoption as sons, the redemption of our bodies. For in this hope we were saved. Now hope that is seen is not hope. For who hopes for what he sees? But if we hope for what we do not see, we wait for it with patience. (Rom. 8:18–25)

I tell you this, brothers: flesh and blood cannot inherit the kingdom of God, nor does the perishable inherit the imperishable. Behold! I tell you a mystery. We shall not all sleep, but we shall all be changed, in a moment, in the twinkling of an eye, at the last trumpet. For the trumpet will sound, and the dead will be raised imperishable, and we shall be changed. For this perishable body must put on the imperishable, and this mortal body must put on immortality. When the perishable puts on the imperishable, and the mortal puts on immortality, then shall come to pass the saying that is written: "Death is swallowed up in victory." "O death, where is your victory? O death, where is your sting?" The sting of death is sin, and the power of sin is the law. But thanks be to God, who gives us the victory through our Lord Jesus Christ. Therefore, my beloved brothers, be steadfast, immovable, always abounding in the work of the Lord, knowing that in the Lord your labor is not in vain. (1 Cor. 15:50–58)

MEANING REINSTATED

*So I hated life, because what is done under the
sun was grievous to me, for all is vanity and
a striving after wind. —Ecclesiastes 2:17*

There was a prisoner-of-war camp in the 1940s where the officer in charge had run out of things for the prisoners to do. So, rather than have them just sitting there planning to escape, he decided to put them to work one day, moving rubble from one side of the camp to the other. The next day, he made them all move it back again to where it had been to start with. The day after that, he repeated the exercise and made them move it across the camp. Then back again. And again, and again. Within a few days, this bunch of captured soldiers started killing themselves: They had been rapidly driven to despair by the sheer futility of what they were doing. Deprived of meaning, even hardened army sergeants couldn't cope.

You and I are not supposed to live in futility. It kills people. And the reason for this is that God designed us to live with meaning, with intention. You may not have noticed this, but the first thing God ever gave Adam, before he gave him animals or commandments or a woman or even clothes, was a job (Gen. 2:15). Think about that: In a perfect world, with no sickness to cure and no dishes to wash up, God gave man a job to do. Why? Because God created us to function best when we have things to do, things which matter, things which have a purpose that honors God and benefits people. It's in our DNA. Meaninglessness stinks.

It always has, by the way. That's why the writer of Ecclesiastes, at least at this point in the story, hates life. People can act as if they're very cutting-edge and original for saying things like "I hate life" on albums or T-shirts, but in doing so they just prove the writer's other point—that "there is nothing new under the sun." Pointlessness has always led to despair. So if you struggle with it and are worried that it might be a 1960s idea that the Bible writers knew nothing about, flick through Ecclesiastes. You might be surprised.

Not only is the statement "all is vanity" not new, it also isn't true. Far from it. Sure, a lucky-dip approach to Ecclesiastes could give you that impression, but if you read the whole thing, you'll find that this is the writer's conclusion of a life *without God*. Getting rich is vanity, he argues; the obituaries in *Forbes* seem to bear that out. Having sex with lots of people is a striving after the wind, he says; just ask the beauty queen five years after you last saw her in *Hello!* magazine. But that doesn't mean that you cannot find meaning. It simply means that you cannot find meaning in the places people usually look for it: wealth, sex, knowledge, power, whatever. If everything "under the sun" is meaningless, then maybe we had better look for meaning somewhere else.

That's where Jesus comes in. Never in human history has anyone lived with such a clear sense of destiny and purpose. Prophesied about before he was born and with a clear understanding of his calling by the age of twelve, Jesus lived like a man on a mission from childhood to resurrection and brushed aside obstacles so firmly he made Winston

Churchill look like a ditherer: "Get behind me, Satan!" "The one who is not against us is for us." "Go and tell that fox … I must go on my way today and tomorrow and the day following." "Leave the dead to bury their own dead. As for you, go and proclaim the kingdom of God." We might think this sort of lifestyle direct or even aggressive, but the one thing you cannot call it is meaningless; the kingdom of God was at hand, and futility and pointlessness had no place there. So while Jesus was inspiring to some, challenging to others, and infuriating to many, he was boring to no one. Life was too short.

And so began the reinstatement of meaning—not just in Jesus' own life, but also in the lives of virtually everybody he touched. Jesus brought, and still brings, an uncountable number of people into his mission to proclaim the kingdom of God. Look at what happened. Deadbeat fishermen became apostles. Tax collectors wrote books that are still best sellers today. Broken, demonized women became the first witnesses of the new creation. Arrogant thugs turned into church planters. By the sheer purpose with which he lived, the man of meaning had taken on futility and won, leaving its wreckage strewn throughout first-century Palestine and giving purpose to generations ever since. Simply by joining him on his mission, millions of middle managers and elderly ladies and self-harming students and disillusioned husbands have had meaning reinstated. They, and we, have had the enormous privilege of knowing the big picture behind God's Word and God's world, what Paul called the "plan for the fullness of time, to unite all things in [Christ], things in heaven and things on earth" (Eph. 1:10). Even when work, family, church, or whatever is a bit pedestrian, there is still a job to do, a kingdom to build for, a world to heal, and a gospel to share.

So don't listen to Marcel Duchamp or Jean-Paul Sartre or the Sex Pistols or whoever else might be telling you that everything is pointless. Because of Jesus, and the kingdom project he kick-started, futility is very, very last season. Meaning is back.

THE RESURRECTION
FROM THE DEAD

*For as in Adam all die, so also in Christ shall
all be made alive.* —1 Corinthians 15:22

Some of the most profound GodStories in Scripture are the most baffling. I don't know why; maybe God made them difficult so we'd have to think about them more carefully. Lots of the big ideas in Christianity are extremely hard to understand—the Trinity, God's choice of us, Jesus as fully man and fully God, and so on. But one that gets less attention than most, despite being very important and very confusing, is the idea that both our death and resurrection take place because we are "in" someone else. If we don't really get this GodStory, then we wobble through life without any real certainty of our future. If we do, however, it's dynamite.

Look for a moment at the first verse we just read: "As in Adam all die, so also in Christ shall all be made alive." This is the sort of sentence we can often just skim over without realizing what it is saying, so we need to slow down a minute. Paul is teaching that we die because we are "in Adam," and that in the same way, we will be made alive because we are "in Christ." What he is saying here, and what he argues in detail in Romans 5, is that we do not die because we sin—we die because we are in Adam. And in exactly the same way, we do not get made alive because we are righteous. We get made alive because we are in Christ.

For people in Western, capitalist, individualistic countries, this is bizarre in the extreme. It sounds like the definition of unfair. Try as we might, most of us cannot understand how we could ever be treated in a certain way because we are "in" someone else; our whole society is built on the basis that you are rewarded or punished because of your behavior, not someone else's. So when it comes to the resurrection, many disciples struggle to be certain that they will be raised from the dead, to an unimaginably glorious and wonderful future with Jesus in the new heavens and new earth, simply because they are in Christ. Therefore many live without an eternal perspective, deciding instead to pursue things that this world has to offer, a bit like an engaged young man sleeping with his ex-girlfriend in case the wedding doesn't work out. Uncertainty leads to ungodliness.

Yet certainty is exactly what Paul has when it comes to the resurrection, because he understands what it is to be "in Adam" and "in Christ." We tend to see the human race individualistically and reckon that us dying because of Adam's sin is like us getting grounded because our older brother crashed the car. But Paul sees the human race organically and reckons that it is perfectly reasonable (and deeply wonderful) for God to treat us as part of a connected whole. Let me illustrate.

If I were to be stabbed in the chest, it would make no difference whatsoever to the well-being of my next-door neighbor, because we are separate and distinct beings. My stab wound would not result in him being short of breath or spluttering or collapsing. But my being stabbed in the chest would make an enormous difference to the well-being of my kidneys and my brain and my left eye. Within a few minutes of me being stabbed in the chest, my kidneys would stop filtering, my brain would stop processing, and my left eye would stop seeing. Human beings are an organic whole, so what happens to one member happens to all the others.

Now, it would obviously be completely ridiculous for a cellular biologist to look at me afterward and say, "How unfair! His left eye didn't get stabbed, yet it died anyway, despite sharing not a single cell with the heart. It was the heart that got stabbed, so the heart is the only bit that should perish." The reason that would be ridiculous is because we all know that the body is a whole. The left eye didn't die because it did something wrong; it died because it was inseparably connected to the rest of me. It died because it was "in Andrew." That is how the Bible views humanity. We don't die because we sin (although we all sin), but because we are "in Adam," so what happened to him happened to us.

But imagine I was rushed to the hospital and resuscitated with a defibrillator, bringing my heartbeat back and supplying oxygen to the rest of my body. My kidney would start filtering, and my brain would start processing, and my left eye would start seeing. Again, our idiotic biologist might look at my eye and wonder why it could see, since the defibrillator went nowhere near my face. But the eye would not be able to see because it had done something—it would only be able to see because it was part of a larger organic whole in which life had overcome death. "In Andrew, all the body has been made alive."

That's where you and I stand in connection with Christ. We will be raised because we are in him, and he has overcome death in himself. There is no doubt here, you see; someone in Christ cannot fail to be resurrected from the dead, any more than my left eye could remain dead while it was part of a living person. What happened to him will happen to us.

That certainty of resurrection is immensely powerful. As long as Jesus' tomb remains empty—and it's been empty for two thousand years—we can have absolute confidence that life has overcome death for anyone who is in Christ, and we can be certain that we will be given new bodies when he returns, life *after* "life after death," to inherit the new creation where there is no suffering or sin or sickness or separation. People who know this live radically. Sure of their resurrection in Christ, they give their time and their finances and their lives for the coming age, and they do so with joy, happily lumping poverty and hardship in the present if it will lead to a more glorious resurrection. They store up treasures in heaven, run in such a way as to get the prize, and suffer with joy because they know what's coming. Listen to Paul's conclusion after his chapter on resurrection:

> Therefore, my beloved brothers, be steadfast,
> immovable, always abounding in the work
> of the Lord, knowing that in the Lord your
> labor is not in vain. (1 Cor. 15:58)

THE FALL OF BABYLON

After this I saw another angel coming down from heaven, having great authority, and the earth was made bright with his glory. And he called out with a mighty voice, "Fallen, fallen is Babylon the great!" —Revelation 18:1–2

The Bible is a tale of two cities. There is Jerusalem: God's city, the city of peace, the joy of the whole earth, the home of God's people. But there is another city, a darker city, that runs alongside her throughout the whole story. This is humankind's city, the city of war and lust and anger and jealousy, of greed, lies, prostitution, violence, and injustice. She wages war to destroy the city of God, from her foundation in Genesis 10 to her destruction in Revelation 18, and she hates God's people and everything they stand for. Her name is Babylon.

She is a master of disguise. Although in her earliest days she was simply a physical city—the city of Babel, founded by Nimrod and home of the infamously smug "tower with its top in the heavens" (Gen. 11:4)—she has continually changed shape, kept up with the times, and wormed her way into every human culture. In the seventh century BC, the geographical city of Babylon was Israel's chief enemy and ended up taking her into exile in three phases, before destroying Jeruasalem and her temple altogether. But when God sent the Persians to wipe out the city, she morphed, like a shape-shifter, into something else; her bricks and mortar were destroyed, but her spirit lived on. In ancient Rome, she fostered lustful, brutal, God-hating paganism, and that is what the early church had to contend with. Ever since, she has stayed sharp, always seducing, always evolving, always catering to whatever sinful desire is in fashion: greed in New York, sex tourism in Phnom Penh, organized crime in Moscow, religious oppression in Mecca, whatever it takes to suck people away from the living God. She loves it.

She loves all forms of idolatry. When people give their lives to money, sex, or power, she is delighted. She had a ball when the French revolutionaries turned Notre Dame into a "temple of reason," and when Wall Street bankers jumped out of windows because they had lost money, and when Nietzsche said that God was dead and humility was a sickness, and when philosophy students read him and fell for it. She loves it when human beings behave as if they do not bear the image of God, which means she is a particular fan of casual sex, self-harm, human trafficking, abortion, and racism. If anything destroys the dignity of people and the worship of God, she will do whatever she can to promote it.

Lined up against her is the city of God, Jerusalem. Like Babylon, she also began as a physical place, but she soon became used as a symbol for all God's people.[1] Like Babylon, Jerusalem has managed to affect human cultures all around the world—in contrast to all other religions, which are still centered on their place of origin (the Middle East for Islam, India for Hinduism, China for Buddhism, Europe for secularism), Jerusalem has flourished in Israel, Turkey, Rome, Northern Europe, and North America, and she is now more influential in Asia and Africa than anywhere else. Like Babylon, she is a spiritual city that has been around since time began. Yet in all other ways, she is the absolute opposite. Where Babylon celebrates idolatry and immorality, Jerusalem is filled with peace, beauty, justice, and the worship of God. No wonder the psalmist calls her the joy of the whole earth.

With opposites like this, you would expect the battle between them to be ferocious. Well, it is and it isn't. Babylon is hell-bent on the total destruction of Jerusalem, that's for sure. She hates God, hates justice, hates Christians, and is out to kill them all (Revelation 17:6 describes her as "drunk with the blood of the saints," for instance). But Jerusalem does not respond in kind. She doesn't fight with swords or Scuds or suicide bombs but with service, building a local church (a Jerusalem) within each and every Babylon, a city within the city that loves it and serves it and preaches the gospel to it. That's why the early Christians, faced with Babylons like Ephesus and Corinth and particularly Rome, formed local churches instead of armies. They knew that the way to defeat Babylon was not by running away from her, nor by shutting themselves in behind their city walls and throwing things at her. It was by burrowing into her as deeply as possible, through love and service, and destroying her idolatry *from the inside*.

There's a great illustration of this in the movie *Armageddon*, in which a meteor the size of Texas is set to hit Earth and wipe out everybody. As NASA meets to work out how to destroy it, an army general suggests firing nuclear weapons at the meteor. The head of research responds that this is a terrible idea, because the meteor is just too big for that. Instead, he argues, what they need to do is to land on the meteor, drill down into it as deep as possible, and then set off the bomb. Because of the bomb's new position in the heart of the asteroid, the entire thing will explode into pieces. The meteor can be destroyed only from within.

That's how Jerusalem destroys Babylon. It's not the church's job to fire her nuclear weapons at Babylon, hoping to outmuscle her or outfight her. Sadly, this is how some Christians think, but it's far from the approach Jesus used. Instead, it's the church's job is to get as deep within Babylon as possible, understanding her culture in order to love and serve people in every city in the world, and liberating others from the evil that oppresses them. That's what William Wilberforce and Martin Luther King and Jackie Pullinger did. That's what Jesus did. That's how the church of God fights, and despite her power, Babylon has no reply to it. She never has, and she never will.

Which is why she is doomed to fall. And so, when Jesus returns, we will see the utter destruction of sick, twisted Babylon and everything she stands for—all her greed, injustice, lust, pride, self-harm, genocide, hatred, and idolatry. On that day, evil will be obliterated once and for all, and the noise of celebration will be overwhelming:

> *"Hallelujah! Salvation and glory and power belong to our God, for his judgments are true and just; for he has judged the great prostitute who corrupted the earth with her immorality, and has avenged on her the blood of his servants." Once more they cried out, "Hallelujah! The smoke from her goes up forever and ever." (Rev. 19:1–3)*

Endnote
1. See for example Galatians 4:26; Hebrews 12:22–24; Revelation 21:2–3.

THE LAST ENEMY

*But each in his own order: Christ the firstfruits, then
at his coming those who belong to Christ. Then
comes the end, when he delivers the kingdom to
God the Father after destroying every rule and every
authority and power. For he must reign until he has
put all his enemies under his feet. The last enemy
to be destroyed is death. —1 Corinthians 15:23–26*

Most thrillers follow the same format. There is a hero, there is a problem to be solved, there is someone to be rescued against impossible odds (usually a lover or a child), and there are a bunch of enemies to be destroyed. Usually there are ups and downs, and if the story is well told, there will be moments when all genuinely appears hopeless, but one by one the hero overcomes the enemies, until there is one left: the big one, the criminal mastermind, the last enemy. This villain usually gets destroyed at the very end; it wouldn't really be the same if Alan Rickman died halfway through *Die Hard*, or if Jack Bauer killed the chief terrorist by eleven o'clock in the morning. The last enemy gets killed at the end because he is the hardest to destroy and the reason all the other enemies are there.

Many GodStories follow the thriller format very closely. Jesus is the hero, the problem is human sinfulness, the people of God are in need of rescue against impossible odds (and wonderfully are

portrayed both as God's lover and God's child), and there are a
bunch of enemies to be destroyed. Temptation is resisted. Sickness
is sent packing in all its forms. Sin itself does not even get a look in.
Demons are dismissed with extreme ease: "Come out of him!" "Be
silent!" Even slightly boisterous storms are told to shut up. As Jesus
approaches Jerusalem, where he will take on the chief villain, we can
look back over a three-year thriller in which all other enemies have
been outmaneuvered and overpowered by Israel's hero. We are now
ready for the final showdown with the last enemy.

That last enemy, the ultimate villain, is death. It first entered
the story back in Genesis 3, and since then it has had a 100 percent
record, crushing all comers. The best and the brightest, the swiftest
and the strongest—not one of them has managed to defeat death.
There has never been a fall in the death rate, no matter what statistics
tell you; penicillin and heart surgery and chemotherapy, as wonderful
as they are, merely postpone the inevitable.

Which all makes Jesus pretty extraordinary. Of course, he
tackled all of death's stooges, if we can call them that, in his earthly
ministry. He fought disease by healing people left, right, and center.
He fought famine by feeding the multitudes, war by teaching people
nonviolence, demons by casting them out, and injustice by standing
up for the poor and the widow. He described his work as the fulfillment
of Isaiah 61, battling against poverty and captivity and bondage and
oppression. He then gave his followers the same mandate. But the
masterpiece of his ministry was the final showdown with death. By
dying and rising again, Jesus took the worst death could throw at
him and still came up smiling. On Easter Sunday, the dominion of
death was broken.

So why do people still die? Surely, if Jesus has fought death and won, we should jump straight into the new heaven and new earth, complete with new bodies, a sin-free world, and the destruction of death altogether. That confused the Corinthians, too. They were puzzled that the resurrection was occurring in two stages—Christ, then everyone else—and wondered if that meant Jesus hadn't risen after all. So Paul explained it carefully.

First, he said, you have to understand that Jesus was the firstfruits of the resurrection, the early crop that guaranteed the rest was coming. There can be a gap between the certainty of something and the completion of something, can't there? Well, Paul says, we are living in between the two. It's like waiting for the harvest when the firstfruits have come through or like waiting for the thunderclap when you've seen the flash of lightning. You know that lightning will certainly result in thunder, and firstfruits will certainly result in a crop, but until it does, you have to wait. It's the same with resurrection: Jesus' defeat of the last enemy means we will definitely be raised, but we're currently still waiting.

Second, Paul argued, death was deliberately being destroyed last so that the kingdom of God could gradually be established over everything: "He must reign until he has put all his enemies under his feet." Death, by divine design, is destroyed at the end, because it is the chief enemy. Jesus could quite easily have abolished death altogether on Easter Sunday and brought about the new resurrection body immediately. But he wanted to establish his kingdom through people, to fill the earth with disciples, and use those disciples to demonstrate his lordship over sickness and famine and war and demons and injustice. He also wanted the maximum number of people to repent and be rescued—so, while people certainly continue to die, they also continue to have lives with opportunities to hear the gospel. Therefore he waited until the latest possible moment, the last trumpet, before destroying death and handing over the kingdom to his Father. Peter made the same point slightly differently:

> *The Lord is not slow to fulfill his promise as*
> *some count slowness, but is patient toward you,*
> *not wishing that any should perish, but that*
> *all should reach repentance. (2 Peter 3:9)*

In the meantime, there is work to be done, to see God's kingdom come over every rule, authority, and power. Death has been dealt a deathblow but is still causing trouble, like a man falling from a skyscraper trying to take as many people down with him as he can. So we have prayers to pray, jobs to do, injustices to fight, sicknesses to heal, demons to cast out, and a gospel to preach while we wait for the rest of the harvest, the thunderclap, the last enemy to be destroyed. That's for starters, anyway …

COFFEE BREAK:

WAIT AND WORSHIP

As the GodStories draw to a close, we find that Jesus has defeated all the enemies, including death itself, and is worthy to be crowned the King of All Kings. This well-known hymn by Matthew Bridges and Godfrey Thring expresses some of the majesty of Christ and should never (in my opinion) be sung quietly. It is a song of triumph, celebrating the collapse of all God's enemies and ours under the conquering feet of Jesus!

> Crown Him with many crowns, the Lamb upon
>   His throne.
> Hark! How the heavenly anthem drowns all
>   music but its own.
> Awake, my soul, and sing of Him who died for
>   thee,
> And hail Him as thy matchless King through all
>   eternity.
>
> Crown Him the virgin's Son, the God incarnate
>   born,
> Whose arm those crimson trophies won which
>   now His brow adorn;
> Fruit of the mystic rose, as of that rose the
>   stem;
> The root whence mercy ever flows, the Babe of
>   Bethlehem.
>
> Crown Him the Son of God, before the worlds
>   began,
> And ye who tread where He hath trod, crown
>   Him the Son of Man;

Who every grief hath known that wrings the
human breast,
And takes and bears them for His own, that all
in Him may rest.

Crown Him the Lord of life, who triumphed over
the grave,
And rose victorious in the strife for those He
came to save.
His glories now we sing, who died, and rose on
high,
Who died eternal life to bring, and lives that
death may die.

Crown Him the Lord of peace, whose power a
scepter sways
From pole to pole, that wars may cease, and all
be prayer and praise.
His reign shall know no end, and round His
piercèd feet
Fair flowers of paradise extend their fragrance
ever sweet.

Crown Him the Lord of love, behold His hands
and side,
Those wounds, yet visible above, in beauty
glorified.
No angel in the sky can fully bear that sight,
But downward bends his burning eye at
mysteries so bright.

Crown Him the Lord of lords, who over all doth
reign,
Who once on earth, the incarnate Word, for
ransomed sinners slain,
Now lives in realms of light, where saints with
angels sing

Their songs before Him day and night, their
   God, Redeemer, King.

Crown Him the Lord of years, the Potentate of
   time,
Creator of the rolling spheres, ineffably sublime.
All hail, Redeemer, hail! For Thou has died for
   me;
Thy praise and glory shall not fail throughout
   eternity.

THE WEDDING

Hallelujah! For the Lord our God the Almighty reigns.
Let us rejoice and exult and give him the glory,
for the marriage of the Lamb has come, and his
Bride has made herself ready. —Revelation 19:6-7

We all live happily ever after. That's how the story ends. Scripture tells us a stormy story of a complicated relationship, and it has more ups and downs than a child on a trampoline, but it all ends well. In the glorious closing chapters of Revelation, it reaches its magnificent climax. The biggest wedding you'll ever see.

It didn't look like it would, though. For much of the Bible, the relationship between God and his people looks like it will end tragically with a messy divorce, not happily with a white wedding. It's a depressingly repetitive story at times: Israel runs off with other gods, God judges her, Israel repents, God forgives, Israel runs off with other gods.

Because of this, the prophets use very strong and sometimes shocking language. They speak of Israel as an adulteress, a prostitute, a cheap whore. Listen:

How the faithful city has become a whore,
she who was full of justice! (Isa. 1:21)

You have played the whore with many
lovers.... You have polluted the land with
your vile whoredom. (Jer. 3:1–2)

Your renown went forth among the nations
because of your beauty.... But you trusted in
your beauty and played the whore because
of your renown and lavished your whorings
on any passerby. (Ezek. 16:14–15)

They sacrifice on the tops of the mountains and
burn offerings on the hills, under oak, poplar,
and terebinth, because their shade is good.
Therefore your daughters play the whore, and
your brides commit adultery. (Hos. 4:13)

The last of these quotations is taken from one of the few men in history who has known how God feels. Believe it or not, God commissioned the prophet Hosea to marry a prostitute, so that he might understand what it was like to experience persistent sexual immorality. It's a horrible and disturbing idea, and it's meant to be, because it shows what Israel was like toward God. Continually, deliberately unfaithful.

But there was a second reason why God told Hosea to marry a prostitute. He wanted to show Hosea how great his love was for Israel, in spite of her unfaithfulness. In passages charged with emotion, God explains that, although Israel's immorality is appalling, his love is so great that he will remain committed to her. Let's be clear: This is not a statement that Yahweh is prepared to work on the relationship, as if it's six of one and half a dozen of the other. It is a statement that, although the immorality is entirely Israel's fault, God's love for her is so overwhelming that he simply cannot abandon her.

It is this unconquerable, incomparable love that makes restoration possible. A child's bedroom wall may be stained with ugly crimson scribbles, but no crayon can withstand repeated coats of paint. And the restoration is completely one-sided. In most romantic comedies, the happy ending is reached by effort on both sides, but not in Scripture. The romance between God and his people is restored by God alone, in Christ alone, through the cross alone. At the cross, in fact, the ceaseless love of God transforms his people altogether, from dirty whores to spotless brides, from graffitied walls to gleaming new paint, in the most movingly romantic action any husband has ever taken:

> *Christ loved the church and gave himself up for her, that he might sanctify her, having cleansed her by the washing of water with the word, so that he might present the church to himself in splendor, without spot or wrinkle or any such thing, that she might be holy and without blemish. (Eph. 5:25–27)*

Can you believe that? We don't come to our senses and clean ourselves up, and God doesn't ignore our filth and decide he can live with it. Instead, he acknowledges our impurity, and then obliterates it. Utterly. He takes all our adultery and whoredom upon himself, remaining faithful even when we are faithless, and clothes us in the purest, whitest garments imaginable. He turns our cheap perfume and tacky miniskirts into a stunning, shining wedding dress. He arranges our hair and adds the perfect accessories. He makes our bloodshot eyes sparkle with delight and our knife-slashed forearms smooth and free from scars. And then, with tears of joy in his eyes as he gazes on the bride his own love has made beautiful, he takes the largest megaphone he can find and says to the world: "Look! My church, the belle of the ball! The most beautiful girl in the world. The bride of Christ."

Jesus is coming back for a wedding. It will be a wedding that makes ours look half-baked in comparison, where the feast will never stop, the wine will never run out, and the dancing will never end. You and I, if we're part of the church of God, will be there—not as a guest, or even an usher, but as the bride herself, the one who cuts the cake and appears in all the photos. So invite all your friends. The wedding is coming soon.

FACE TO FACE

For now we see as through a glass, darkly; but then face to face. —1 Corinthians 13:12 KJV

My wife, Rachel, gave me permission to tell the story of when she accidentally went to the bathroom in front of a whole bunch of people at a dinner party. We were at a friend's house for dinner with a number of others, all of whom we knew, but none very well. Just before dinner, Rachel went to the bathroom, which was at the end of the corridor. She did what all of us would have done: She walked in, shut the door and bolted it, and sat down. She noticed nothing unusual. She then saw the rest of the dinner party wandering along the corridor toward the kitchen. Again, nothing. Then suddenly, the thought occurred to her: Why can I see those people? How could that be possible? It then hit her like a punch in the stomach. If I can see them, then they can see me. You see, for some reason, our friends had used clear glass on their toilet door, with a blind that was sometimes up and sometimes down. On this occasion, it was up. You can imagine her panic. Our friend saw what was happening and leaped to her aid, blocking the door so that no one else could see her. But it was too late. A dinner party had seen Rachel going to the toilet, and the result was extreme embarrassment (for her) and extreme laughter (for everyone else). She had assumed she was looking "through a glass, darkly" but was actually visible "face to face."

When Paul wrote 1 Corinthians, he was not talking about frosted glass on toilet doors. He was probably referring to the polished bronze mirrors that Corinth was known for producing, which tended to distort and blur the image when they got old and dark. But you get the idea. There is a massive difference between seeing someone through a glass darkly, and seeing them face-to-face. When you see someone through frosted glass, or in a dark and faded bronze mirror, you can work out their shapes and their colors but not their exact detail. You might be able to tell that a person was female and wearing a pink sleeveless top but not that she had green eyes, mascara, and dimples when she smiled. For that, you would need to see them face-to-face.

This is how Paul describes the contrast between knowing Jesus now and knowing him when he returns. For now, we see him in a limited fashion, through a glass darkly—enough to make out the shapes and colors and to give a general impression, but nothing like enough to give an accurate description. (In context, Paul is arguing that this is why prophecy and tongues and knowledge are good for now, but have limitations.) When Jesus comes back to reign, however, and renews the heavens and the earth, and gives resurrection bodies to all who love him, we will see him face-to-face, without any of these limitations and hindrances. We will know him fully, not just in part. Just think about that for a moment, because it has two wonderful implications.

The first is that mystery is okay. If you're anything like me, you want answers to everything: the Trinity, sovereignty and free will, suffering, the millennium, and who killed JFK. But in many cases, we're not supposed to have all the answers—because we are looking through a glass darkly—and that's all right. We can make out shapes and colors of God's character and purposes, and he has revealed an awful lot of it, but it's never going to be as clear as we would like it to be. In fact, it's very good for us to have a sense of mystery when approaching the living God, and it certainly doesn't hurt us to shrug our shoulders every now and then, because it means we have to acknowledge our limitations.

The second implication is far more exciting, though, and it blows my mind. Even the most profound revelations of Jesus we have now are mere sketches, silhouettes, dim reflections of what he is actually like. That's incredible. I find Jesus a fairly captivating and awe-inspiring person as it is, so the idea that the Jesus of the Gospels, and even the Jesus of Revelation, is being seen through a glass darkly is phenomenal—and it makes me wonder what on earth seeing him face-to-face will be like. If the love of the Jew from Nazareth is through a glass darkly, what kind of love will we encounter when we see him face-to-face? If the power that stilled the storm is a misted image on a bronze plate, what will his power look like when we meet the real deal? And if people fell before him in delighted awe when the glass was opaque and frosted, what will we do when the glass is removed altogether? I can only imagine.

Yet that's where the GodStories are headed. Remember, Paul knew a fair bit about the revelation of Jesus; he knew his Old Testament backward, then met the risen Jesus himself, then spent thirty years healing and preaching and raising the dead in Jesus' name. If anyone was entitled to think they had Jesus sorted out, it was Paul. But the closer he got to Jesus, the bigger Jesus became, and the more Paul realized there was much more to know. So he looked forward to Jesus' return with all his being, while keeping a sense that he would never quite get his head around it.

So can we. We can celebrate the incomprehensible wonder of Jesus for now, yet with trembling excitement that we are only scratching the surface, like a couple who love being engaged but know that it's pointing forward to an even greater future. We can delight ourselves in the range and depth of his GodStories, all the while suspecting, as C. S. Lewis put it, that we are only really in the table of contents page, and that the real story is yet to start. We can try to wrap our heads round the incomparable God and his unfathomable gospel—the story beneath the story and the gospel of the glory, shame removed and earth renewed, redemption and reconciliation—yet admit, with happy humility, that we really don't know what we're talking about. And we can preach GodStories with passion and joy, yet recognize that even on our best days we are looking at the one who wrote them through a frosted pane, a glass darkly.

That's Jesus. The lion and the lamb, the lifeboat and the scapegoat. The barnstorming, star-forming, ocean-making, trespass-taking Lord of the world. And one day we will see him face-to-face:

> *No longer will there be anything accursed, but the throne of God and of the Lamb will be in it, and his servants will worship him. They will see his face, and his name will be on their foreheads. And night will be no more. They will need no light of lamp or sun, for the Lord God will be their light, and they will reign forever and ever. (Rev. 22:3–5)*

THE GOSPEL OF GOD

Now after John was arrested, Jesus came into
Galilee, proclaiming the gospel of God. —Mark 1:14

Every story has a hero. And every GodStory has the same hero. Let's conclude by reminding ourselves of who he is.

He is the universe's creator, Adam and Eve's template, and the serpent's nemesis. He condemned Cain and accepted Abel. He was the destroyer of the earth in floodwaters but the rescuer of Noah and his family. He is the initiator of covenants, the inventor of the rainbow, the confuser of man's speech, and the confounder of man's arrogance. He is Abraham's shield and his very great reward, the maker and keeper of outrageous promises, and the God who calls by grace and justifies by faith. He provides Isaac's substitute. He stands in the middle of Jacob's brook and at the top of Jacob's ladder, and turns a wheeler-dealer into the father of a nation. The giver and fulfiller of Joseph's dreams and the One who works for good what man had intended for evil, he saves a man, a family, and an entire empire.

He is the God of the burning bush: Yahweh, I am who I am, the God of Israel. He is Moses' salvation, Aaron's inspiration, Miriam's celebration, and Pharaoh's nightmare. It was he who destroyed Egypt with a river, healed Israel with a branch, and crushed Amalek with a staff, so when he tells Israel they are to have no other gods but him, you had better take notice. He is in the cloud by day, the fire by night, the glory mist in the tent, the thunderstorm on the mountain, the water from the rock, the flame that consumes Nadab and Abihu, and the earthquake that swallows Korah. So unstoppable are his purposes that the rent-a-prophet Balaam is physically unable to speak against his people.

He is the commander of the army of Yahweh, producing the courage of Joshua, the refuge of Rahab, the parting of the Jordan, and the collapse of Jericho. He is the song of Deborah, the sword of Gideon, and the strength of Samson. He opens Hannah's womb and Samuel's ears, and his ark alone—the box in which he lives—is enough to smash the Philistines, break their gods in pieces, win battles, and conquer cities. He is David's rock, his shield, his fortress, his hiding place; yet he is also the forgiver of his sins and the restorer of his joy. To Solomon, he gives wisdom and wealth. To Elijah, he is the widow's oil, the Carmel fire, and the still, small voice. To Elisha, he makes the dead live, the leper clean, and the axe head float. He is Jehoshaphat's ambush, Hezekiah's deliverer, Sennacherib's conqueror, Josiah's lawgiver, Ezra's teacher, Nehemiah's confidence, and Esther's rescue. In other words, he is the hero of every story in the entire Old Testament.

And not just the stories. In Job, he is the truly sovereign One whose purposes are unsearchable and whose power is too wonderful to fathom. In 150 psalms spanning a thousand years, he is the hope in every situation and the answer to every cry, not to mention the praise of every song. Isaiah's Holy One of Israel, Jeremiah's righteous branch, Ezekiel's Yahweh-who-is-there, and Daniel's revealer of mysteries are all one and the same. Not only that, but the prophets then reveal God as Hosea's faithful Father, Joel's outpoured Spirit, Nahum's vengeful warrior, Jonah's merciful judge, Zephaniah's rejoicing husband, and Zechariah's conquering King. By the time you finish Malachi, you cannot help but feel somewhat exhausted at the variety of the GodStories and the majesty of their hero. The whole thing is, quite literally, the gospel of God.

Then Jesus steps in. If you were impressed before, you can only stand amazed now as the man from Nazareth embodies the story of God to perfection. The supporting cast reflect the brilliance of the hero by their remarkable range of reactions to him: overjoyed shepherds, a jealous king, a confused John the Baptizer, a loyal (but often even more confused) band of followers, exasperated Pharisees, overjoyed tax officials, furious temple leaders, welcomed prostitutes, frustrated militants, forgiven sinners. As God provides his clearest demonstration of what he is like, the human race is not sure what to make of him, but the GodStories continue. He is Nicodemus's answer, Legion's defeat, Lazarus's life, Caesar's alternative, Thomas's proof, and Peter's restoration. Finally, he is the defeat of sin and death, and in his crucifixion and resurrection he lays the foundation for the gospel of God to go global.

With the pouring out of the Holy Spirit, the stories multiply. No longer confined to a physical body, or even to a single ethnic group, our hero starts popping up all over the place, often at the same time. Luke's breathless account in Acts makes a valiant attempt to get it all down on paper—Barnabas's generosity, John's faith, Ananias's death, Stephen's conviction, Philip's evangelism, Paul's conversion, and the rest—but, like a six-year-old trying to get the football from

Ronaldinho, he cannot keep up with the ever-expanding GodStories that spring up from Antioch to Azotus, and ends his account with our hero still healing bodies and saving souls. As Acts finishes, the gospel of God is ongoing. And it still is.

So the whole Bible is about God. It is full of stories in which he is the main character, the climax, the resolution, and indeed the author. The writers of Scripture, as much as they were interested in human beings and earthly events, were incapable of writing narratives, poems, prophecies, or visions that weren't about God. In fact, so much is he the purpose, the hero, and the punchline of all stories that to talk about anything else would be to miss the point completely, like focusing on the frame of the Mona Lisa or the grass in front of the Taj Mahal. "For from him and through him and to him are all things. To him be glory forever. Amen" (Rom. 11:36).

Welcome to the gospel of God.

APPENDIX: A WORD ABOUT POSTMODERNISM

This appendix is not for everyone. If you don't know what postmodernism is, or if you don't care, then you've finished the book already. But this may clarify a few things for (1) those who think postmodernism is the most terrible thing imaginable and that no one in this generation will now believe the real gospel. And it may also have something to say to (2) those who think postmodernism means no one believes in truth these days and that we need to continually reinvent the gospel while steering clear of terms like absolute truth, sin, repentance, and so on. So there should be something in this appendix to annoy just about everybody.

Against (1), I believe that if we understand postmodernism, it will present us with massive opportunities for the gospel. I don't think there's anything to be scared of at all, and in fact, churches that hold fast to the gospel theologically while engaging with (and learning from) postmodernism culturally are likely to see significant success in this generation. That's what I mean by fixed theology and flexible culture; Paul's passage on food offered to idols in 1 Corinthians 8—10 is a classic example of how to do both together.

Against (2), on the other hand, I think that a critical engagement with postmodern ideas will show us that we don't need to reinvent the gospel at all, even if we need to rethink some of the ways we communicate it. Sadly, some churches have misunderstood postmodernism to mean that the old gospel won't work now, so we need to try a new one. But any Jesus we preach has got to be the Jesus of the four gospels, not the decaf Jesus of post-1960s Western liberal mythology.

Interestingly, both (1) and (2) display the same confusion. Both assume that the gospel of the Bible cannot be preached in a way that postmodern people will respond to. With (1), this fear often results in simply returning to a "modernist" way of preaching and interacting with the culture, while with (2), it results in jettisoning some crucial aspects of biblical teaching. Both may have a certain appeal in some quarters, but neither will be much use to the church, let alone the lost culture it is there to rescue. And both, perhaps surprisingly, misunderstand what postmodernism actually is.

By itself, of course, the word *postmodern* simply means "after the modern period," which is a fat lot of use. Maybe that's why there is so much confusion about what it is. In our culture, however, the word *postmodern* is used to mean three different things, which overlap but are not identical. Let's look at them briefly.

Pop Culture Postmodernism

This is the everyday variety of postmodernism, which more than anything else describes a style of speech, and particularly humor. This may sound trivial, but it is probably the most wide-reaching aspect because it is so accessible. Pop culture postmodernism shows itself in conversation and humor that are laden with irony, self-aware to the point of self-mocking, and with a tendency to jump in and out of the surreal: basically, anything from *Monty Python* to *Flight of the Conchords*, from *Wayne's World* to *The Office*. Conversations in the postmodern generation are marked by an almost continual note of self-parody, and comedy is more likely to come from something you say about yourself than about someone else. Overall, this sort of humor is probably the single most coherent way in which we can refer to anything like a "postmodern generation"—you get it, your parents don't quite, and your grandparents don't even realize it's meant to be funny. In itself, this is not a huge issue for presenting the gospel, except in provoking us to communicate more effectively.

Intellectual Postmodernism

At the opposite end of the obscurity spectrum there is intellectual postmodernism. Although the church has tended to react with horror, or at least suspicion, to anything that smacks of this, there is actually a lot to learn from it. We may well reject most of the conclusions of Lyotard, Derrida, Foucault, and Rorty—and I do—but despite that, postmodern philosophy has done a lot of good, challenging some rather naive modernist views about knowledge, history, progress, and meaning. In particular, it has contributed two observations, both fairly uncontroversial.

The first is that the modernist story of progress is at best exaggerated and at worst downright dangerous. Modernism is supposedly the story of gradual improvement; as humanity comes of age, it reaches maturity and learns how to solve its problems. Look at the terms we use: We had a Renaissance (suggesting new life, in contrast to the dead and dreary medieval period), and then we had an Enlightenment (suggesting light, in contrast to the previous darkness). At one point, people even spoke of the "new age" as opposed to the "middle age," but two world wars quickly consigned that to the intellectual dustbin.

Each of these terms has the same effect. They suggest that since the discovery of the steam engine or electricity or natural selection or democracy, humanity has been freed from the darkness of superstition (and religion) and is making a beeline for the light. Knowledge has overcome ignorance, sickness, and poverty, and it's just a matter of time before strife and war—and death?—disappear with them.

To which postmodernism says: Really? Does the last hundred years fit with that account of history? Obviously, we would concede a small part of it. Science *has* made us better at postponing death, the global population has grown, and many of us now have more possessions and more freedoms than we used to. But the problem with all this is that there seems to be no parallel between the advance of scientific discovery and the advance of human goodness, let alone happiness. The darkness-to-light fable of modernity might sound convincing from the life-expectancy statistics or the suburban shopping malls of Western Europe or North America, but it didn't in Ypres or Hiroshima or My Lai, and it still doesn't in Gaza or Abu Ghraib or the Parisian *banlieues* or downtown Detroit. Nor does it ring true for the millions of ordinary homes where post-enlightenment families, with good education and quality health care and the right to vote and an Internet connection, are ground into misery and fracture by greed, pornography, selfishness, loneliness, or abuse. So perhaps modernism's story is a bit overblown—maybe you can enjoy electricity and democracy without assuming that the Western countries who found them will inherit the earth and live happily ever after. Perhaps modernism's story is part of the problem, not part of the solution, in places like Vietnam and Afghanistan and Iraq. Perhaps it's time to consider some other stories. And that presents an opportunity for preachers of the gospel. Who knows? Those stories might even include GodStories.

The second punch postmodernism has thrown at modernism, which overlaps with the first, is that there is no such thing as neutrality. Everyone has a viewpoint, postmodernists tell us, and no one is able to see the world from nowhere. So rather than repeating our version of the one big story, we should open ourselves to the possibility that there are other perspectives, that other people's stories might be as useful as ours or even more so.

That doesn't mean they are all equally valid, of course. Not even the most diehard postmodernists would say that two completely contradictory statements could both be true. But there is an important idea here, which as Christians we would do well to learn from. There is a journey we need to go on as we interpret events, texts, and even Scripture, through dialogue with people who don't share our worldview. In the long run, this will help us understand the Bible better—particularly since there are cultures in the world today that are closer to the biblical ones than ours—and communicate it more helpfully.

Now there is a lot of junk in postmodern philosophy as well. It's obvious that, despite some philosophers, texts *do* convey meanings of their own (a point which, presumably, these philosophers concede as soon as they write a book intended to convey meaning). It's equally clear that although people can often use words to exercise control over people, not all speech takes place in the service of oppression (or, once again, the philosophers who say so would be doing exactly the same thing). It should also therefore be obvious that every text in the Bible has a meaning and that it is possible to find out what it is (even if we don't like it). And so on. But we mustn't throw the baby out with the bathwater. Postmodernism contains some helpful ideas, and if we are prepared to learn from them, we may be able to share GodStories and interpret the Bible more effectively.

Cultural Postmodernism

Finally there is the (ever so slightly mythical) cultural postmodernism, which often appears more in the eye of the beholder than in reality. To listen to some Christians, you would think that ever since Derrida, or even Nietzsche, people in the West have agreed that there is no such thing as truth or meaning, and therefore, that convincing people the gospel is true has become all but impossible. In the case of (1), this can mean despairing of ever seeing evangelistic fruit. With (2), it can mean reinventing evangelism so that churches say nothing about the truth of the gospel.

Now, to be fair, there are a few silly people who say that there is no such thing as truth; if you meet them, you can usually ask them "Is that true?" and be done with it. But the vast majority of people don't talk like that. They may well be pluralistic, in that they believe society is safer when we allow everyone to believe what they like as long as they don't harm others. They may not believe in a "religious" truth and in fact may blame such ideas for most of the world's evils. But they will still believe in truth. In many cases, they will actively preach the gospel of education or economic growth or science or tolerance—"the gospel of the glory of the blessed free market," perhaps, or "if you confess with your mouth that learning is Lord, you will be saved."

Richard Dawkins and Sam Harris and Christopher Hitchens and

almost every other famous atheist believes in truth.[1] They might not believe what is *actually* the truth, but that doesn't mean they don't believe in truth. They do. So do the people on your street, whether or not they would call it that. At root, therefore, secular pluralism is not saying that all worldviews are as true as each other but that all religions are as bad as each other. Therefore postmodern people need to hear exactly the same message as the pagans Paul preached to in Athens and Ephesus and Corinth: God is one, Jesus is risen from the dead, and that changes everything.

Conclusion

So disciples of Jesus have nothing to fear from postmodernism. At a pop culture level, it means people's conversation and humor have changed, but that just means we need to talk differently and make different jokes. At an intellectual level, it provides a welcome rebuttal to the dominant worldview of the eighteenth to twentieth centuries, and it may even have a lot to teach us about handling Scripture. And at a cultural level, I think it exists more in the minds of frightened believers than in reality and requires exactly the same gospel to be preached, even if we need to get better at telling it in different ways.

At the end of the day, if postmodernism forces us to tell different GodStories, then that won't be such a bad thing. It worked in Acts. It will work again.

Endnote

1. Richard Rorty, a world-renowned philosopher who argues that philosophy should be about solving practical problems rather than pursuing "truth," nevertheless points out that virtually nobody believes there is *no* truth (*Truth and Progress: Philosophical Papers* [Cambridge, UK: CUP, 1998]).